# THE
# VISIBLE
# EXPERT<sup>SM</sup>

How to create industry
stars. And why every
professional services
firm should care.

I went from being an in-house expert to a globally recognized speaker in just a few years. I can personally attest to how useful increasing your personal brand can be to your career and to your company. If you are looking to promote your personal brand, increase your company's revenues, or become a well-known expert in your field, you should read this book in its entirety. It will give you all the information you need to become a Visible Expert.

- **Brad Geddes**, Founder of Certified Knowledge

*The Visible Expert* is an unparalleled resource to guide you to become just that — a truly visible expert. If you want to grow your business, the knowledge, experience and detailed information in this book is an absolute must have!

- **Jay Niblick**, Bestselling author of *The Profitable Consultant* & Founder of Innermetrix Incorporated

Being an expert in a vacuum gets you nothing. To make your mark, you need to define your area of expertise and share it in multiple venues. If you are an expert who wants more, this is your A-Z guide.

- **Mark Amtower**, leading government marketing consultant, speaker, and best-selling author

*The Visible Expert* is an invaluable tool for any professional services firm that wants to differentiate itself in today's extremely competitive world. Hinge has researched how buyers of services view experts and how visible expertise results in measurable financial benefits. I highly recommend this book to all business owners that are looking for an edge in winning new clients and growing their business.

- **June Jewel**, CPA, President & CEO, Acuity Business Solutions and author of the Amazon #1 bestseller, *Find the Lost Dollars: 6 Steps to Increase Profits in Architecture, Engineering, and Environmental Firms*

The professional services world is awash in content, and so remarkable insight—like what I see in *The Visible Expert*—is such a breath of fresh air. The research-based, carefully articulated concepts in this book are unusually helpful.

- **David C. Baker**, author, consultant, and principal of ReCourses

What's the nature of experts' value? Can you classify experts? How do you find them, grow them? *The Visible Expert* takes these questions seriously and provides answers that are sure to be useful to any professional services firm.

- **Charlie Green**, Named a Top 100 Thought Leader in Trustworthy Business Behavior

A great perspective on Visible Experts and their impact on their companies and on society at large. Directly addresses key issues on most professionals' mind. A must read for young professionals.

- **Tony Bansal**, Internet Executive & Entrepreneur

This book is a battle-tested field guide for taking your expert status to the next level. Read it, live it, and crush your competition!

- **Tim Ash**, CEO of SiteTuners, bestselling author of *Landing Page Optimization*, and chair of the Conversion Conference

The Visible Expert, Copyright © 2014 by Lee W. Frederiksen, Ph.D.,
Elizabeth Harr, Sylvia S. Montgomery, CPSM
Emily Paterson, Editor

Published by Hinge Research Institute
12030 Sunrise Valley Drive, Suite 120
Reston, Virginia 20191

ISBN 978-0-9904459-0-6

Printed in the United States of America

**Design by Hinge.**

Visit our website at www.hingemarketing.com

# THE
# VISIBLE
# EXPERT<sup>SM</sup>

How to create industry
stars. And why every
professional services
firm should care.

Lee W. Frederiksen, Ph.D.,
Elizabeth Harr,
Sylvia S. Montgomery, CPSM,
and Emily Paterson, Editor

# Contents

# Acknowledgments

Writing a book whose authors also have demanding day jobs is an exercise in collaboration. While only three names appear on the cover, an entire team of researchers, editors, designers, and project managers worked behind the scenes to make this book happen. This chapter is dedicated to those rising stars.

First, we would like to thank our tireless editor, Emily Paterson, who turned our drafts and partially articulated ideas into a coherent and easy-to-read manuscript. This book would have been much different (and shipped much later) without her extraordinary talents and diligence. She sacrificed many weekends to bring this work to fruition.

We also want to express our appreciation to our partner, Aaron Taylor, who added value at every stage. His perspective and ear for language made this book more polished and engaging.

John Tyreman was essential to the collection, organization, and interpretation of the data behind our findings. His analytical skills and proficiency with a spreadsheet allowed us to make the connections and uncover the insights at the heart of this project.

We would also like to appreciate Brian Lemen, whose exceptional eye for design made the book a delight to read. He prepared the print version of the book and its electronic incarnations.

To Candace Frederiksen, who interviewed the vast majority of the Visible Experts in our study, we owe our sincerest gratitude. And many thanks to Janice Maida, who spoke to the rest.

Without Lindsay Nichols, we never could have pulled off such an intricate undertaking in such a short time. Her talent as a project manager was put to the test as she deftly herded the cats that are our team to a satisfying conclusion.

We would also like to thank designers Christian Baldo and Shikha Savdas for designing and producing the book's handsome charts, as well as Kristin Claeys who provided design support at several critical junctures.

Finally, we would like to offer our sincerest thanks to the hundreds of participants in our study, including the seventeen experts we spotlight in the text. Without the benefit of their experiences our journey to the summit would never have begun.

# Introduction

Every day, we read, watch, and hear from experts in our field. When the media needs an expert's perspective, they reflexively reach out to these individuals. They are widely admired, and they seem to turn up everywhere you look.

Did you ever wonder how these folks made it big? Are they just smarter and more energetic than the rest of us? What's the secret to reaching as wide an audience as these industry stars?

At our own firm, these questions have been percolating for a long time. So we decided to find some answers. First, we gave these industry stars a name. We called them Visible Experts<sup>SM</sup>. Then, we got to work. We set up a study of 130 Visible Experts and over 1,028 buyers of their services. By looking at both sides of the equation, we would learn not only how these stars grew to prominence, but also why buyers preferred them over less well-known experts.

In this book you'll learn that Visible Experts ascend to celebrity in stages, and that they use a common set of skills and tools to get there. You'll see that some individuals rocket to the top in record time — as much as five times as fast. And you'll learn what these Fast Trackers do differently. Best of all, you'll find out that firms that develop Visible Experts are better known, attract more leads, and grow faster.

So hold on! You're about to learn not only how others reached the top, but also how you and your colleagues can get there, too. Along the way, you'll hear from real-life Visible Experts who share their stories and advice for those who want to follow in their tracks.

Strap on your crampons and grab your ice axe. We're headed up the slopes.

Visible Experts follow a similar path to success, regardless of their backgrounds.

# The Power of the Visible Expert<sup>SM</sup>

**CHAPTER 1:**

# What is a Visible Expert<sup>SM</sup>?

CEO and founder of the Content Marketing Institute, Joe Pulizzi is known in the marketing world as the Godfather of Content Marketing. As he took the stage during the first Content Marketing World conference in September 2011, an event for which he had worked nonstop for the previous 18 months, it seemed like he had grown into the title. "They're announcing my name, and I'm walking out onto the stage to deliver the keynote," he says. "Everyone's clapping. Almost a thousand people from 27 different countries have traveled here, to my event, to hear what I have to say. I look out over the crowd and everything's quiet. And that's when it hits me: I've really made it."

## Introducing the Visible Expert<sup>SM</sup>

In every industry, a few stars shine a little brighter than the rest. We all know who they are. They're the folks everyone loves to quote and namedrop. The men and women who keynote the biggest conferences. The ones with the TV

Visible Expert<sup>SM</sup> is a service mark of Hinge Strategy LLC interviews and books. We call these industry stars Visible Experts — professionals who have attained high visibility in the marketplace and a reputation for expertise.

Visible Expert: A professional with high marketplace visibility and a reputation for expertise.

When we compare these Visible Experts to ourselves and our own careers, it's easy to get discouraged. Their achievements and status can feel out of reach. They must be different, we think. Super smart. Or maybe just lucky.

But in most cases we'd be wrong. In fact, the vast majority of Visible Experts we interviewed for this book insist they are no more intelligent or lucky than any other business person. As Joe Pulizzi, perhaps the most prominent name in content marketing, says, "At the end of the day, I'm not smarter than anyone else. I just didn't give up, I found a niche where I could distinguish myself, and I worked really hard."

Then how did these experts become so successful and so visible? We just had to find out.

## The Research

In the first-ever study of its kind, the Hinge Research Institute interviewed 130 Visible Experts and surveyed 1,028 buyers to discover how these stars got where they are today (see Chapter 2 to learn more about our research).

In the process, we discovered that the benefits of being a Visible Expert extend beyond individuals to their firms and peers. This phenomenon is known as the *halo effect*.

The *halo effect* transfers the benefits of a Visible Expert to their firm.

## What is the Halo Effect?

In 1915, a researcher named Edward Thorndike conducted a study to learn how people judge each other. He discovered that if a person had one strong positive trait—such as being attractive—it would positively influence the rater's perception of that person's other traits. Intelligence or work ethic, for instance, tended to be rated equally as strong. Thorndike called this phenomenon the halo effect. Subsequent studies determined that the same effect applies to businesses, which explains the importance of marketing and brand-building activities.

For Visible Experts, the halo effect means that a buyer who sees an expert in a positive light is likely to believe that the expert's firm is wonderful, too. In this way, Visible Experts elevate their firms in every category that counts, including growth, new business, reputation, partnerships, billing rates, and the ability to close sales. Staci Riordan, partner at the law firm Fox Rothschild and pioneer

Visible Experts help firms increase reputation, partnerships, billing rates, and new business.

of the fashion law sector, puts it this way: "People hire the person, not the firm. So the stronger the individual, the stronger the firm will be. It's a symbiotic relationship."

The research is clear—when Visible Experts rise to the top, they bring their firm along for the ride.

## The 5 Levels of Visibility

Not all Visible Experts have reached the same level of visibility—and not all of them want to or need to. Certain industry stars, like Warren Buffett or Bill Gates, are so visible that their fame has expanded beyond their industry, attracting the attention of the mainstream public. Other Visible Experts are beginning their ascent—and their reputations within their industry are just starting to catch fire.

According to Rick Telberg, founder of CPA Trendlines and a Visible Expert for the finance sector, experts must think strategically about goals and growth before they start. "The professional services industry is a lifestyle sector," says Rick. "Experts must decide how much they want to earn and how much they want to work. Then they shape their business around that."

There are five Visible Expert levels.

Between the novices and the Warren Buffetts, our research revealed a wide range of visibility, as well as certain tendencies that appear at turning points along the way. Five natural levels emerged, each defined by its own set of criteria. We'll dive into these levels in Chapter 3, but here's a sneak peek:

**Level 1: The Resident Expert**
Though recognized as an expert by clients, staff, and colleagues, they are not well known outside of the firm.

### Level 2: The Local Hero

Their expert brand is starting to be known beyond the boundaries of the firm, occasionally attracting new business. They are starting to engage in promotional activities such as speaking engagements and blogging.

### Level 3: The Rising Star

Reputation is moving onto the regional or even national stage, attracting better business and higher fees.

### Level 4: The Industry Rock Star

These experts have become nationally recognized names within their niches, driving top-tier business opportunities and commanding premium fees for themselves and their firms.

### Level 5: The Global Superstar

These elite experts have garnered considerable exposure outside their niches. In some cases, their names have become synonymous with their areas of expertise, and major firms clamor to be associated with them.

## The Journey to the Top

Once we uncovered these five levels of visibility, it became clear that most experts were using surprisingly similar tactics to rise from level to level. Despite their varying career choices, they were adhering to a similar process, and the process is what got them where they are today.

As we analyzed our findings, we discovered a small subset of Visible Experts who were moving to the top more quickly. We call this group the Fast Trackers. Now, the Fast Trackers were doing all the same things as other Visible Experts to build their expert brands—but they were doing some very important other activities, too.

Here's the really exciting part: using what we learned about Visible Experts and Fast Trackers, we were able to break down the process into a clear and replicable program. For the first time, professionals don't have to guess how to rise to the top of their industry. Using data from real-world experts as your guide, we're going to show you not only how to get to the top, but also how to do it *faster*.

*What are we waiting for? Let's begin!*

# Ian Brodie

In 2007, Ian Brodie left the consulting world to start a solo practice, helping those in the professional services attract new clients and grow their businesses. In six short years he has become a Visible Expert in online marketing, known for helping clients achieve 50-100% growth in a single year. Along the way, he's won multiple awards and written a book, *Email Persuasion*, which became a #1 bestseller on Amazon.

Ian credits his quick rise to the power of content marketing. The secret to launching yourself as a solo practitioner or small business, he says, is quite simple: "Create 'leveragable' content. Then share it and nurture it. And repeat. When leads start to trickle in, find ways to nurture and connect with them." For Ian, email marketing has been the best way to nurture the leads that find him through his blog and other channels. In fact, Ian says, other than content marketing, "I don't do any other business development, and no networking. People find me through my blog and social media."

Ian also likes to remind his clients: "It doesn't need to be perfect the first time." Sometimes professionals become paralyzed by the idea that something has to be perfect, so they never take that first step of starting a business or creating a piece of content. "When you allow yourself to learn as you go," Ian says, "you take a lot of pressure off yourself. Remember that it's a process, and try to enjoy the ride."

## TAKEAWAYS

- Visible Experts are professionals who have attained high visibility in the marketplace and strong specialized expertise.

- Firms can benefit from their in-house Visible Expert's fame through a phenomenon called the halo effect.

- There are five Visible Expert levels, each one defined by unique criteria.

- Across a wide range of industries, most Visible Experts use similar tactics to get to the top.

- A subset of the experts we studied, which we call Fast Trackers, were able to reach the top much more quickly than other Visible Experts.

- That process is replicable, and this book will show you how to do it.

# Sarah Susanka

When she launched a firm with her partner at the age of 26, architect Sarah Susanka was already bucking the status quo. Unlike most major architectural firms, which made the bulk of their profits on major commercial projects, Sarah focused exclusively on the homeowner market. Sarah and her partner created a whole new business model, making a name for themselves at home and garden shows and other events where their target audience was likely to attend.

By 1996, Sarah's firm had grown to 45 employees and was one of the most sought-after firms in Minnesota. Then she wrote her best-selling first book, *The Not So Big House*, which redefined the notion of "home" and became a cultural touch-point for a generation interested in sustainability and community. Almost overnight, Sarah was launched into the spotlight, fielding media requests and being interviewed by heavyweights like Oprah, Charlie Rose, and Diane Rehm.

These days, although she still designs houses, Sarah spends much of her time sharing her ideas through lectures and writing (she's written eight more books). She has been featured on Good Morning America, CNN, NPR, HGTV, and This Old House, and has been called upon for her insights on culture and design by *USA Today*, *The Wall Street Journal*, and *The New York Times*. Always an architect at heart, Sarah has found a way to define her career through an entire cultural movement—one created by herself.

# CHAPTER 2:

# The Research

As a firm that works with professional services firms, we have conducted a lot of research over the years—for our clients and on the industries we serve. We noticed that many firms seemed to benefit from the celebrity of their most prominent experts—apparently driving company growth and profits. This got us to wondering if this phenomenon was common. And if so, could we understand how it works? This book is the product of our quest to answer those questions.

## Prior Research

After conducting research for a previous book, *Inside the Buyer's Brain*, we knew that buyers place a high premium on reputation and expertise when selecting a professional services provider. We also noted that many high growth firms had highly visible professionals who were an integral part of their company. The role of those experts in building a professional services firm's reputation, combined with their visibility, pointed the way to new research.

During our collaboration with RAIN Group on the second edition of *Professional Services Marketing,* we uncovered evidence that achieving a certain level of expertise can affect company growth. Curious, we began looking around for more evidence. While books and articles that draw on interviews with individual experts are plentiful, we couldn't find much research on large groups of industry experts. How had they achieved success? What benefits did they convey to their firms? In Chapter 1, we described how Visible Experts produce a halo effect, transferring benefits to their firms through association. But we wanted to know *how*. To answer all of these questions, we needed to conduct our own research.

> This book offers first-of-its-kind research on Visible Experts.

So we developed our own study of prominent experts in the professional services, dubbing them Visible Experts. Our study included a systematic, quantifiable study of over 100 Visible Experts and over 1,000 buyers of their services. As far as we know, it's the first study of its kind—a comprehensive examination of industry experts and what it takes to become one.

## So Many Questions

In *Inside the Buyer's Brain,* we discovered that expertise and reputation are the two most important reasons clients select a firm. So we asked ourselves: what's the best way for a firm to demonstrate it's as good as it claims? Well, nothing proves expertise like having an actual expert on staff. And a famous expert? That just magnifies the appeal. As we dug deeper into these Visible Experts, we knew we had tapped into something valuable.

> Nothing proves expertise like having a famous expert on staff.

## Research Design

From our previous research on the professional services industry, we knew that it was critical to look at an issue from both the provider's side and the buyer's side. Providers would tell us how Visible Experts achieved their status, while buyers would reveal how clients look for services and what characteristics they value most. Comparing the two sets revealed insights and opportunities.

We studied Visible Experts and the clients who hire them.

## Visible Expert Interviews

First we studied the Visible Experts. Using a combination of personal interviews and secondary research (reviews of biographical information, social media tools, and other expertise indicators), we studied 130 individuals who are recognized experts in their fields. For research candidates to qualify as Visible Experts, two independent sources had to endorse them as experts. The interviews used a combination of open-ended questions and 0-10 ratings. The participants' open-ended responses were coded into categories, which we then analyzed and used to make comparisons.

"The research interview was an unusually worthwhile interaction. The interviewer went well beyond the usual data-only questions, and got me to discuss deep questions of motivation, lessons learned, and good practices going forward. This kind of discussion is not normally found these days, and considerably raises the average quality of business interviews."

**– Charles Green,** CEO and founder of Trusted Advisors Associates and Visible Expert for the consulting industry

During the interviews, we asked the Visible Experts open-ended questions in two primary categories.

1. We asked them how being a Visible Expert has affected various aspects of their business, including lead sources, billing rates, partnership opportunities, and closing new business.

2. We asked them about their career path. How long did it take them to become a Visible Expert, and what steps had they taken? Which tools were the most valuable in getting them to the top? What would they have changed? And what advice do they have for others?

We conducted comprehensive research on 130 Visible Experts.

## Buyers' Survey

On the purchaser's side, we surveyed 1,028 buyers of Visible Expert services, using an online survey with multiple-choice responses, where participants could select all that apply.

### *We wanted to know:*

- Why do buyers hire Visible Experts?

- What challenges do Visible Experts help solve?

- How do they find Visible Experts?

- What convinces the buyers of their expertise?

- What are the perceived benefits from working with Visible Experts?

We looked at why and how buyers select Visible Experts.

## The Results

Once we collected the data, we began to analyze it. This required coding the responses, collating the data, and looking for patterns and trends. When the analysis was complete, two remarkable findings rose to the top:

- Firms with upper-level Visible Experts were receiving benefits across almost every metric.

- Most Visible Experts had followed a similar path to success, regardless of their industry, education, or training.

Visible Experts follow a similar path to success, regardless of their backgrounds.

In the next chapter, we will take you on the journey to Visible Expert success, showing you what happens at each stage as visibility increases. *Fasten your seatbelt—it's a wild ride.*

## TAKEAWAYS

- This book seeks to answer three major questions:

    * What are the benefits of being a Visible Expert—for the individual and the firm?

    * What does it take to become a Visible Expert?

    * Is the process replicable?

- Using a mix of surveys and secondary research, we studied 130 Visible Experts and 1,028 purchasers of professional services, comparing the two sets to uncover insights and opportunities.

- The research indicated that upper-level Visible Experts reap benefits for their firms in almost every metric.

- Most Visible Experts follow a similar path to success, regardless of their industry, education, or training.

# Jay Baer

Jay Baer, president of the digital marketing consulting firm Convince and Convert, didn't set out to become one of the world's top social media and content marketing experts. At the time, his best friend was diagnosed with cancer, and Jay realized that life was too short to spend doing something he didn't love. So he set off on his own, launching and selling one successful firm before founding Convince and Convert in 2008.

Jay turned a profit in his first month on his own, and he has never had an unprofitable month since. Part of his success is due to his networking talents. "My network was built on chicken wings and Bud Light," Jay says. "There's no substitute for getting out there and working hard and meeting people." He picked up three clients in the first week and hasn't looked back since.

Jay has turned communication into a specialization. For clients, he is the ultimate translator, taking complicated technology and marketing concepts and turning them into practical, easy-to-explain business principles for companies around the globe. He says, "I'm in the *understanding* business, and I was able to figure that out really early."

Jay's advice to entrepreneurs is to learn to say *no*. He says, "Every year we come up with a list of 15% of activities that didn't get us ahead, and we stop doing them. The trick to running a successful business is to figure out what you are uniquely qualified to do—and then do only that."

CHAPTER 3:

# The Journey

Nobody is born a Visible Expert. Like all of us, they started out unknown. Many of them experienced business failures. They had doubts. They questioned themselves. Then, somewhere along the way, they found a niche and established themselves as experts. As their skills matured, these individuals developed strategies to make the most of their expertise. And their reputations began to grow.

Visible Expert Tim Ash is a case in point. He experienced several valleys and peaks before founding Site Tuners, a company focused on website conversion rate optimization. Tim's wife met him when he was leaving one startup to found another. He had invested everything in his idea, and launching his firm required an 18-month period when he took no salary. "I wasn't the best date, since I had to be picky about where I could afford to eat," Tim jokes.

> Visible Experts focus on different challenges at each level.

He chalks up his success to a combination of stubbornness, industry expertise, a very supportive wife, and a high tolerance to risk. "My parents are immigrants from Russia. They left everything behind to bring my brother and me here when I was eight years old," says Tim. "So the model of risking everything and working hard for success was natural to me."

Tim is a great example of someone who has worked his way up the ladder of visibility. In fact, our research reveals five distinct levels of visibility, each defined by its own set of criteria. At each of the five stages, experts focus on different aspects of their careers, use different tools for self-promotion, face different challenges, and enjoy different benefits. There are also certain things that some Visible Experts do to rise faster. We will discuss these Fast Trackers further in Section 2.

In this chapter, we look at the entire ascent of the Visible Expert, from novice to international superstar, exploring the changes, challenges, tools, and achievements Visible Experts experience in the course of their ascent.

## Level 1: The Resident Expert

Before you become a Visible Expert, you must first establish your expertise. Level 1s — Resident Experts — are focused on establishing themselves as thought leaders and experts within their firms. For this reason, Resident Experts put a strong emphasis on self-education and on improving their skills. Indeed, their only regret is not investing in themselves and their careers sooner.

Resident Experts depend on their firms to attract new business.

Just ask international marketing consultant, Ian Brodie. According to Ian, becoming a Visible Expert "starts with figuring out what to be an expert in. This should be a combination of what you know, and what people need. The next step is developing outstanding content—something substantial and useful—and figuring out the best ways to get the content to your audience."

Although their firm's leadership has recognized their value, Level 1s are not yet visible, or are barely visible, outside of their firms and the clients with whom they work. For the most part, Resident Experts depend on their firms, repeat client work, and occasional word-of-mouth referrals for business development. Their emerging visibility among clients and colleagues has only just begun to generate new business.

Beyond building expertise, many Resident Experts have not begun to specialize. Figure 3.1 shows how specialization is attractive to buyers, making it easier to differentiate providers in the marketplace. Sellers' lack of a niche is an obstacle that Level 1s will need to overcome as they become more visible and grow their reputations.

**Level 1 at a glance:**

Low visibility outside firm

Focus on self-education and building expertise

Firms generate new business for them

Not specialized

Low use of promotional tools

**Figure 3.1** What Buyers Value (from *Inside the Buyer's Brain*)

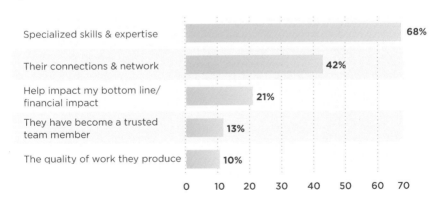

Specialized skills & expertise — 68%
Their connections & network — 42%
Help impact my bottom line/financial impact — 21%
They have become a trusted team member — 13%
The quality of work they produce — 10%

0  10  20  30  40  50  60  70

Many Resident Experts are heavily involved with client work and have not focused on promoting their *expert brand*. For the most part, they are using neither digital tools—such as blogs, emails, and social media—nor offline tools—such as articles, public speaking events, and partnerships—to boost their visibility.

Resident Experts focus on client work rather than promotion of their *expert brand.*

## Level 2: The Local Hero

Level 2s, or Local Heroes, have begun to think strategically about their careers. They are realizing that they should share their thought leadership outside of their firms and engage in more promotion. With their newfound visibility, Local Heroes begin contributing in a significant way to company growth and their firm's ability to close sales. Their firms are starting to rely on them to bring in new business.

Local Heroes are starting to specialize and build visibility outside the firm.

Unlike Level 1s, Local Heroes are starting to specialize. In fact, Level 2s say the most important thing they've done is to focus on a target market, and many wish they had found a niche sooner. They are experiencing the power of differentiation in the marketplace.

Chris Mercer, Visible Expert for the finance industry and the founder and CEO of Mercer Capital, explained his early struggles like this: "In the beginning, we couldn't afford to turn down a quarter million dollars in bank consulting work, but that wasn't what I wanted to focus on. I realized that we were getting spread too thin and needed to specialize. Within three years we dropped consulting and focused exclusively on our valuation business. And that's been our primary niche for over 20 years."

Local Heroes begin to engage strategically in promotional and marketing activities. They use basic digital tools to promote their expert brands, favoring blogs, content outlets, LinkedIn, and webinars in particular. They begin attending networking events and speaking at local conferences, even if the venues are not always a perfect fit for their area of expertise. The number of partnership opportunities grows significantly, so they have to be more selective about which partners they choose. And as they become more visible, partners are starting to seek them out.

Differentiation and promotion are paying off— Local Heroes begin bringing new business to their firms on the strength of their own names. Although they still rely mostly on referrals, other lead sources come into play for the first time. These include speaking engagements, interviews, social media, and websites.

**Level 2 at a glance:**

Starting to build visibility outside firm

Focus on specializing and finding a niche

Rely on referrals to generate new business

Begin using speaking engagements, social media, and websites to promote their expert brand

23

## Level 3: The Rising Star

Level 3 is the tipping point for Visible Experts. At this level, we see entrepreneurial risk taking, a strong focus on a niche, and frequent use of tools to promote an individual's expert brand. Level 3's Rising Stars can reach a larger audience and they are recognized as market leaders. Their firms now rely on them to bring in business and are starting to reap rewards for being associated with their name.

Rising Stars focus on entrepreneurial risk taking, specialization, and promotion of their expert brand.

The Rising Star's firm is reaping big benefits from its association with a Visible Expert. The firm enjoys growth, new leads, and the ability to close more sales as a result of the Rising Star's reputation. Some Level 3s begin reassessing their fit with their firm.

**Level 3 at a glance:**

Visibility is growing fast

Focus on entrepreneurialism and promotion

Their firm now relies on them to bring in business and close sales

Strong emphasis on blogging and social media tools

Rising Stars understand that communicating their message and leveraging marketing tools—including blogging and social media—are critical to building their reputations.

Visible Expert Lori Randall Stradtman, for instance, used blogging, social, and online marketing tools to take her social media consulting business to the next level. A first-adopter of social platforms, Lori blogged regularly and was active on social networks from the early 2000s. "I was vocal in a community of people on social media that liked me and would share my stuff," she says. "Then I started a podcast for authors, where I got them to share their lessons-learned."

Word quickly spread that Lori was a social media guru. Soon she was being asked to host conferences, lecture at universities, and submit articles to major mainstream media outlets. As a result of all of this exposure, Wiley Publishing invited her to write a book for their famous Dummies series. The book, *Online Reputation Management for Dummies*, cemented Lori as a Visible Expert, allowing her to work with much bigger clients and to raise her fees fivefold.

Level 3s also experience an increase in speaking inquiries, and the venues are of a higher caliber. As more partners seek them out, these Visible Experts are able to choose among prestigious partners, building strategic relationships.

Rising Stars' firms are reaping big benefits from their association with a Visible Expert.

## Level 4: The Industry Rock Star

Level 4's Industry Rock Stars have passed the tipping point. Like a snowball rolling down a hill, their visibility has taken on a life of its own and continues to generate new opportunities. They no longer need to chase down speaking engagements, media mentions, partnerships, or new business. Instead, the challenge now becomes managing and filtering the flow of inbound leads and partnerships. Whereas Level 3 was all about generating buzz, now the word is out, and activities focus on refining and managing that reputation.

Industry Rock Stars' firms rely on them for new business and closing sales.

"Writing my book caused a cascade effect. I started receiving requests for speaking and lectures. Then someone saw me lecturing and asked me to do a TED talk. The TED talk led to a profile in *The New Yorker*, which led to even more opportunities. All of this led to a great surge in new business."

— **Robert Lang,** engineer, internationally known origami artist, and owner of Lang Origami.

Although inbound leads increase across every level, experts see the biggest increase in inbound leads at Level 4. Now experts turn their attention to being selective and choosing clients who are a good fit. With a strong and highly visible reputation, Industry Rock Stars experience a big jump in the percentage of sales they close. As their reputations continue to expand, these experts' names become more closely tied to their firms, generating greater growth and profitability.

Industry Rock Stars' visibility takes on a life of its own, generating more leads than they can easily handle.

In Level 4, promotional and marketing activities move into a wider sphere. The Rock Star's name is starting to become widely recognized in the industry, requiring less online promotion.

Instead, there is a new and greater focus on keynotes, books, and writing whitepapers and articles. Industry Rock Stars are also much more likely to receive speaking requests than lower-level experts. Search engines continue to be an important source of new leads, and Rock Stars rely on Google Alerts and other tools to monitor what the media and others are saying about them.

Visible Expert Charles Green, CEO and founder of Trusted Advisor Associates, is a perfect example. As his visibility has grown, he no longer needs to invest in advertising or outgoing

# Charles Green

Charles H. Green has turned trust into a business. A public speaker, author, and founder of Trusted Advisor Associates, Charles teaches organizations how to build trust, improving both client relationships and sales.

Charles' trust in his own vision gave him the confidence to leave the consulting world after 20 years with the goal of writing a book. He did not have a concrete idea in mind, but, he says, "I had confidence in my instincts. I did things that made sense to me, and they turned out right nine times out of ten."

The book that emerged was *The Trusted Advisor*, co-written with David Maister and Robert Galford. Designed to help professional services leaders improve client relations and increase sales through trust, the book became a huge hit, catapulting Charles to Visible Expert status.

Instead of advertising or outbound selling, Charles has used content marketing to expand his visibility. Today, Charles generates valuable, mostly free content on a consistent basis. This practice builds both his reputation and his already wide visibility. When CEOs want to learn even more, they are willing to pay for his services because they already trust him—once again, it all comes back to trust.

Charles points out that becoming a Visible Expert requires self-confidence, self-trust, and an open mind. If you want to be successful, he says, "find the thing you can do really well, and do the hell out of it." Great words to live by.

**Level 4 at a glance:**

High visibility within their industry

They often generate more new leads than they can handle

Firm relies heavily on them for business and closing sales

New focus on keynotes, books, and writing whitepapers or articles

selling. His brand is so big that people seek him out, rather than the other way around. Although he eschews advertising, Charles continues to promote his name through different types of content marketing. Putting out valuable, mostly free content on a consistent basis allows Charles to continue to grow both his reputation and his already wide visibility. When industry leaders want to learn even more, they are willing to pay for his services because they already trust him.

## Level 5: The Global Superstar

Level 5 Visible Experts, which we call Global Superstars, have entered an intense level of visibility. Their names have become their own brands and they are now recognizable both inside and outside of their industry. The Global Superstar's biggest challenge is filtering and selecting: leads, partnerships, and new business opportunities. Many of them employ gatekeepers to manage their time.

Firms that partner with a Global Superstar receive multiple benefits from their association.

Firms that partner with a Level 5 receive many benefits from their association. Companies receive advantages across all metrics that we studied, including brand recognition, reputation, trust/credibility, market leadership, closing sales, and fees.

Global Superstars find that speaking engagements, TV interviews, articles, search engines, and books are their best lead generators. The importance of blogs and social media diminishes even more at this stage, continuing a trend that started in Level 4. Since a Global Superstar is already so well known, online brand promotion and marketing are far less necessary. In a sense, mainstream media channels have become a Level 5's blog—they are doing the expert's broadcasting and promotion for them. After all, the media are happy to snag an interview with a Global Superstar—their words sell papers and earn clicks.

When Visible Experts reach Level 5, their names have become their own brand, and they are able to build a company or launch a product on the strength of their reputation alone. Priorities shift, and reputation management becomes more important than expanding visibility. A damaged reputation can really hurt a Global Superstar's market value. Warren Buffett, CEO of Berkshire Hathaway and Global Superstar for the financial sector, understands the critical importance of protecting reputation at this level. At Warren's level, his name has become synonymous with that of his firm, and a black mark against the man or the firm will hurt both.

**Level 5 at a glance:**

Visibility has expanded outside industry

Can launch a company or product on the strength of their name alone

Receive so many business opportunities that filtering is now a challenge

Rely on speaking engagements, TV interviews, articles, search engines, and books for promotion, while social media and blogging are less important

Global Superstars are recognized both inside and outside of their industry.

In a memo to his managers, Warren wrote, "We can afford to lose money—even a lot of money. But we can't afford to lose reputation—even a shred of reputation. We must continue to measure every act against not only what is legal but also what we would be happy to have written about on the front page of a national newspaper in an article written by an unfriendly but intelligent reporter."

As Warren Buffett knows, Global Superstars are under a public microscope and must be careful about preserving reputation and presenting a consistent message. Architect and author Sarah Susanka learned the same lesson after she was launched into the limelight with the publication of her best-selling first book, *The Not So Big House*. Suddenly, she found herself juggling multiple high-profile media requests, including interviews with Oprah Winfrey, Diane Rhem, and Charlie Rose.

For Global Superstars, blogs and social media become much less important.

Becoming a Global Superstar means that Sarah is now able to create and shape industry trends. "Once, I had an interview with *The Washington Post*," Sarah says. "I made an offhand comment about something my husband and I had been talking about the night before. The next day, I opened the newspaper and there was my offhand comment! The thing that I had talked about suddenly became a trend." This incident made Sarah realize how careful and strategic she needed to be. "Now when I get interested in things, the press follows because they want to know: what is the next big thing? It's heady stuff."

## Visibility and Prosperity

With every increase in visibility, a Visible Expert garners more media attention, more (and better) partnerships, and a higher level of clientele. If you assume that they also make more money, you would be right. That's exactly what the data revealed. In the next chapter, we will explore the benefits of attaining Visible Expertise—for individuals and their firms. And we'll explore the effects on business as visibility increases.

## TAKEAWAYS

- There are five levels of visibility, and each level brings different focuses, challenges, tools, and achievements.

- Level 1s are Resident Experts whose value is recognized by clients and colleagues but are not well known outside of their firm. They are focused on skill development.

- Level 2s are Local Heroes working on increasing their visibility. Their reputation has moved beyond the firm and they've started attracting business.

- Level 3s, or Rising Stars, have moved onto the regional or even national stage, using a variety of self-promotional tools to attract partners and clients at higher fees.

- Level 4s are Industry Rock Stars. Famous within their industry, they attract top-tier business opportunities and command premium fees for themselves and their firms.

- Level 5s are Global Superstars whose names have become synonymous with their areas of expertise. They convey major benefits to firms that are associated with their name.

# Robert Lang

When Robert Lang started making origami art at the age of six, he never thought that it would one day launch him onto the international stage. But, over time, origami became increasingly important to this engineer-artist. And while he earned a Ph.D. in applied physics and took a job developing laser technology, Robert was also publishing books of his origami designs on the side.

After a decade of engineering, Robert was ready to merge his hobby with his engineering career. "I had already published seven books teaching people how to replicate my origami designs," he explains. "Now I wanted to teach people how to create their own." This was a major move—something that had never been attempted.

The book that came out of that decision, *Origami Design Secrets: Mathematical Methods for an Ancient Art*, is considered to be Robert's magnum opus, and it pulled him into the limelight, cementing his status as Visible Expert. "There were increasing requests for lectures," he says. "Someone would see me at a lecture, and it would turn into another project. Eventually I got asked to do a TED Talk, which led to a *New Yorker* profile, and so on. It became a cascade of visibility."

Today, Robert receives more requests for work than he can accept, from designing products that fold onto themselves to making art for TV commercials. How does he select projects? He says, "Before I sign on to a project, I ask myself 'am I going to enjoy this?' Personal satisfaction has always been a primary driver." This criterion could be seen as a defining philosophy for Robert's entire career. "I set out to do interesting things, things that were fun and personally satisfying. I became a Visible Expert almost by accident."

# CHAPTER 4:

# How Visible Experts Benefit Their Firms

By now, you've learned how Visible Experts rise through the ranks, progressively increasing their prestige and attracting new business. We've also discussed how the halo effect can pull the expert's firm into the spotlight. But can we measure the value to a firm of having a Visible Expert on its team? The answer is an unqualified yes.

When we studied the impact these stars have on their firms, we got pretty excited by the data. From generating leads and closing sales, to attracting better clients and partners, Visible Experts were having a major effect on growth and profit. In fact, the research showed Visible Experts accruing benefits for their firms across almost every metric. In this chapter, we'll walk you through the key findings so you can see for yourself.

> Visible Experts play a major role in driving growth and profit for their firms.

## Visible Experts: Overall Effect on Firms

To determine Visible Experts' impact on their firms, we first asked our experts an open-ended question: what effect, if any, did their increased visibility have on their firms as a whole?

*Over 60% of our experts reported two major benefits:*

1.  An expansion of their firm's brand-building capabilities, and

2.  An increase in their firm's overall growth and business development.

These figures become even more impressive when you consider that among our respondents were Level 1 and 2 experts, many of whom are not yet experiencing the effects of their visibility. Let's explore the impact of each of these two major benefits.

### 1) Brand Building

Almost sixty-two percent of Visible Experts said they substantially contribute to building their firms' brand. When we looked at specific brand-building activities, we learned that having a Visible Expert on staff helps firms establish market leadership and credibility, boost their firm's reputation, and heighten brand recognition in the marketplace. Firms also enjoy increased brand awareness simply by being associated with a Visible Expert's name. Figure 4.1 tells the whole story.

62% of Visible Experts accrue brand-building benefits for their firms.

**Figure 4.1** Visible Experts' Impact on Firms' Brand-Building Capabilities

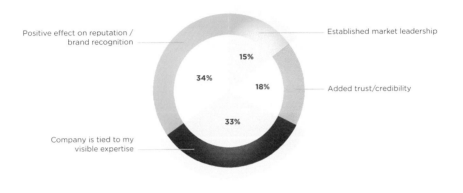

Positive effect on reputation / brand recognition

Established market leadership

15%

34%

18%

Added trust/credibility

33%

Company is tied to my visible expertise

## 2) Growth and Business Development

A lawyer who had grown up in the fashion and clothing industry, Staci Riordan recognized the huge need in the fashion industry for lawyers who intimately understood the business needs of fashion and garment companies. In 2006, she started the country's first fashion law practice at Thelen, LLP. When Thelen folded in 2008, she accepted an offer at Fox Rothschild, bringing all of her fashion clients with her and founding the firm's Fashion Law Practice Group. "Fox Rothschild is a perfect fit," Staci says. "It's a very entrepreneurial environment, and they foster creativity." A little more than seven years after becoming a member of the bar, Fox promoted Staci to equity partner—a rare occurrence in today's market. The firm encourages Staci to do what she loves: helping clients in the fashion industry build their businesses. In the process, they reap the benefit of having a highly visible partner—one whose name is synonymous with fashion law—promoting the firm's brand far and wide.

66% of Visible Experts accelerate growth and business development for their firms.

Staci's experience is not uncommon. Sixty-six percent of Visible Experts reported playing a major role in their firms' growth and business development, with the greatest effects occurring in firm growth, lead generation, and audience reach. Experts also helped firms command premium fees and close sales. All of these factors add up to accelerated growth and business development.

Next, we'll dig into some of these subcategories.

## Impact on Firms' Lead Generation

It turns out that Visible Experts are powerful engines of new business. Not only do firms with a Visible Expert on staff experience a significant surge in inbound leads, but Visible Experts also permit firms to be more selective when screening those leads, and they make it easier to close new leads after you've screened them.

Visible Experts are powerful engines of new business.

*Visible Experts employ a variety of methods to produce leads:*

- Content production—blog posts, articles, whitepapers, and books
- Speaking engagements—including keynotes, webinars, podcasts, and interviews
- Networking activities and relationship building
- Search engine marketing
- A focus on target markets

Next, we looked at what happened to these lead-generating activities as our stars moved from level to level.

## Driving Leads Through Speaking Engagements and Search Engines

In Chapter 3, we saw how the importance of some lead sources—such as blogging or books—changes from level to level. But two lead sources remained consistently important across the entire spectrum of visibility, driving many more leads as experts rose to prominence. These two sources were speaking engagements and search engines. The data showed a clear trend: as Visible Experts become more visible, these two channels continue to generate more new business for their firms.

> Speaking engagements and search engines are important lead generators at every level of visibility.

Jay Baer, President and founder of the digital marketing consulting firm Convince and Convert, discovered early on that speaking engagements are a huge lead generator. So he invests a lot of resources in this channel, averaging 60 live speaking events and 25 webinars per year. Last year, he spent

48 weeks on the road, mostly in North America—but also globally. "I love traveling," Jay says. "But the opportunity cost is definitely higher for international events, with the logistics, the time away, and the time changes." Jay also cohosts a podcast, Social Pros, which is paid for by sponsors. Each week, he and his cohosts interview a different social manager for the big brands. This approach not only drives visibility, but it also gives Jay insights into what the big players in the marketplace are doing.

**Figure 4.2** Visible Experts Identifying Search Engines as a Lead Source

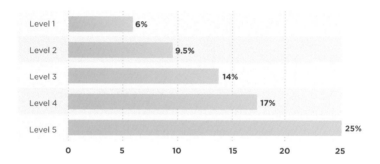

**Figure 4.3** Visible Experts Identifying Speaking Engagements as a Lead Source

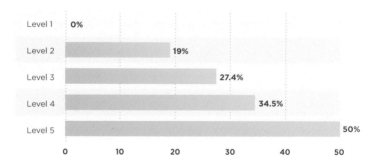

# Chris Mercer

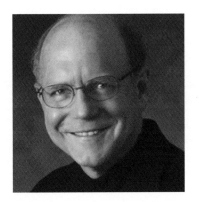

When he was a young man working for the investment firm Morgan Keegan, Chris Mercer made a name for himself as a valuation expert, appraising businesses for merger and acquisitions and litigation. "No one wanted to do it, so I took it on as an 'extra,'" he says. "Then I began to realize that there could be a business in there."

So, in 1982, Chris left to start his own valuation practice, Mercer Capital. He set up shop with an Osborne 1 computer with a tiny screen and a Smith Corona printer that took five minutes to print a single page. "Unlike other self-employed consultants, I kept my salary to where it was at Morgan Keegan," Chris says. "And any extra cash flow, I invested back into my business."

Long before the Internet, Chris used content marketing to expand his visibility through writing, speaking, and newsletters. Over time, he realized that his strategy needed targeting. "I made a diagram of all the subject matter that we had sent out, along with our target clients," he says. "And I realized that we were not sending out any specific topics consistently to any specific audience." So he made changes to his newsletter, and it has been a huge hit. He still emails it to thousands of clients and prospects each quarter.

Books were also an important piece of Chris's content marketing strategy, giving his firm the clout to compete with big-name accounting firms. Chris notes, "If a prospect hires Mercer Capital, an unknown, it is a bigger risk. We needed to be known and be perceived as being big and being thought leaders. The books put us on the map as a valuation company."

## Billing Rates of Visible Experts

Next we looked at a subject near and dear to many in the professional services industry: billing rates. We had anticipated that buyers would be willing to pay more for a Visible Expert, but we had no idea just how much more. The study revealed that buyers are willing to pay over 13 times more for a Level 5 Visible Expert than for a regular professional!

**Figure 4.4** Relative Hourly Rates Buyers Will Pay, by Visible Expert Level

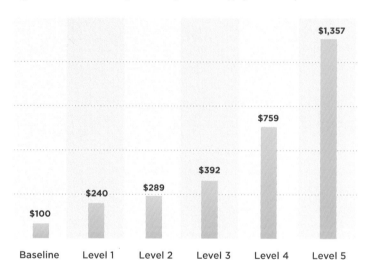

In fact, Visible Experts of every level command premium rates, starting at over 200% of the baseline for a Level 1 Visible Expert. And as an individual's level of visibility increases, the rate rises dramatically. The numbers speak for themselves—having a Visible Expert allows firms to command the highest industry rates.

Buyers are willing to pay over 13X more for a Level 5 Visible Expert

This certainly rings true for Visible Expert Charles Green, CEO and founder of Trusted Advisors. Charles left the fast-paced word of consulting after 20 years, starting his own firm and writing a book on trust-based consulting. After the success of his book launched him into the spotlight, Charles increased his fees by 150%. Later, he was able to double his fees after joining a speaker's bureau, an organization that books all of his public speaking engagements.

*Visible Experts of every level command premium rates.*

## Marketplace Demand for Visible Experts

In previous research, we had discovered a generalized demand for high-profile expertise among professional services buyers. This time we went a step further, measuring marketplace demand for Visible Experts by level of visibility.

**Figure 4.5** Buyer Demand (% of Buyers) for Visible Experts by Level

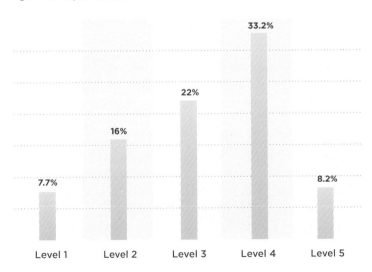

| | |
|---|---|
| Level 1 | 7.7% |
| Level 2 | 16% |
| Level 3 | 22% |
| Level 4 | 33.2% |
| Level 5 | 8.2% |

Interestingly, the data reveals that demand for expertise rises consistently with an expert's level of visibility—then abruptly decreases at Level 5. Why? While the data didn't provide a definitive answer, this drop-off probably occurs because relatively few business challenges call for international-level experts. Remember, too, that Level 5 experts command much higher fees—almost double the hourly rate of a Level 4 expert. Purchasers are realistic about the scale of their needs and will choose a more affordable Level 4 expert when the services of a Global Superstar are not truly required.

So when might a client need a Level 5 expert? Here's just one example:

When chain department store Target was trying to make a name for itself in the 1990's, it had a problem: how to differentiate itself from the competition. Walmart already had the reputation for rock-bottom prices—what could Target do to stand out? The situation called for a Level 5 Visible Expert. Enter Michael Graves, a famous architect who had already had won more than 100 awards for architecture and design, and whose portfolio included major projects around the globe.

> Demand for expertise rises consistently with an expert's level of visibility.

Target partnered with Michael Graves, trading on his already strong brand to bring an aura of sophistication to the store. The partnership was a huge success, lasting 13 years and creating a model for many other retail-designer relationships for years to come. The relationship was a win-win for both parties: Target became known for a sophisticated level of style and design, and Michael Graves' visibility grew even more. As a result of this single partnership, he would be forever known as the man who believed in "good design for all."

If you are a managing executive, the results make a strong case for cultivating a Visible Expert in your ranks. But does the demand drop-off at Level 5 mean you should not pursue development of a Global Superstar? Not necessarily. This is a strategic decision, one you should make based on your firm and your market. Remember that while demand drops off at a Level 5, service fees go way up—each engagement brings in much more revenue. Questions such as "who is your audience?" and "are you trying to take your firm global?" will help you determine how high your Visible Experts need to go.

## Visible Experts + Professional Service Firms = Growth and Profit

Visible Experts shape their firms in powerful ways, guiding brand development, driving growth, attracting better clients and partners, and making it easier to close sales. And the higher their level of visibility, the more these stars benefit their firms.

**Figure 4.6** Percent of Visible Experts that Impact Their Firm's Brand

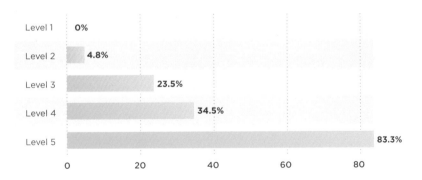

In fact, a high-level Visible Expert can actually "make" a firm, transforming its brand and propelling it to new heights of success. Bottom line? For professional services firms, hitching your wagon to a star is a smart business move.

## TAKEAWAYS

• From generating leads and closing sales, to attracting better clients and partners, Visible Experts play a major role in driving growth and profit for their firms.

• 62% of Visible Experts contribute to firms' brand-building activities, and 66% of Visible Experts accelerate growth and business development for their firms.

• While Visible Experts employ a wide variety of methods to generate new business, speaking engagements and search engines are important lead generators at every level of visibility.

• Visible Experts command premium rates, starting at over 200% of the baseline for a Level 1 expert. Buyers are willing to pay over 13 times more for a Level 5 Visible Expert than for a regular professional.

• Buyers' demand for expertise rises consistently with an expert's level of visibility, falling off when the Visible Expert becomes an elite global superstar.

# Joe Pulizzi

When it comes to content marketing, Joe Pulizzi wrote the book. In fact, he's written three of them. As founder and CEO of the Content Marketing Institute (CMI), which he started in 2010, Joe was one of the first marketers to define and implement the concept of content marketing, and it's possible that he even coined the phrase.

Like many Visible Experts in our study, Joe says that becoming an author was a turning point in his career, opening doors that otherwise would have remained locked. After publishing his book, Joe found himself being asked to speak at increasingly bigger events. He was invited to contribute to a special author series, and major clients, such as LinkedIn and SAP, were attracted to his firm. The snowball effect is typical of Visible Experts that use content marketing. And today, CMI receives so many inbound leads that his team has to turn away business.

When Joe is not helping large corporations with content marketing training and strategy, you'll find him blogging, working on a book, or giving keynotes. In the midst of all of this activity, he also found time to launch Content Marketing World, an annual conference that drew over 1,700 participants last year. The event is so popular that his team has now added a sister conference in Sydney, Australia.

For others wishing to become a Visible Expert, Joe has this advice: "Think strategically. Have a vision. Niche yourself as small as possible. And prepare to work really hard."

# CHAPTER 5:

# The Client's Perspective

The data showed us that Visible Experts produce a halo effect for their firms, causing an increase in almost every important business metric: reputation, inbound leads, partnerships, closing sales, and fees. But we still didn't know why this happened.

Why do buyers value Visible Experts? How do they find and engage Visible Experts, and what benefits do clients find in working with them? To find out, we went to the source. As part of our Visible Expert study, we surveyed 1,028 buyers of professional services. Here's what we discovered about the buying process.

> We surveyed over 1,000 professional services clients.

## Buyers Want Visible Experts to Solve Problems

Clients most often seek out a Visible Expert when they have a specific problem or challenge. They need a solution fast, so they call in the big guns.

But buying decisions are a bit more complex than that (see Figure 5.1). In our study, each buyer listed an average of 2.4 reasons for seeking Visible Expert services. The reasons fell into four general categories:

### 1. To solve a critical problem
Time constraints (urgency), the need to solve a high-impact problem, and a lack of internal expertise were common reasons for seeking out a Visible Expert.

### 2. To build the brand and win new business
Buyers want to attract new clients and tap into new markets—and they seek out an expert with high visibility to help shape their brand and leverage their reputation and industry profile to bring in new business.

### 3. For the confidence conferred by an expert
*We feel more comfortable working with a well-known expert. We want to work with the best.* These sentiments illustrate a powerful psychological phenomenon among buyers: engaging an expert gives the buyer confidence and peace of mind.

### 4. For a legal proceeding
The final and least common category is also the most specific: engaging an expert to testify in a legal proceeding.

**Figure 5.1** Why Buyers Seek Visible Experts

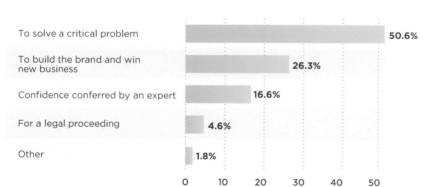

# Buyers Use a Variety of Methods to Find Visible Experts

After need is established, buyers begin the search for a Visible Expert. They search online. They read articles and other thought leadership pieces. They ask friends and business partners. In some cases, they are already familiar with an expert. After searching—usually in multiple ways—they compile a list of finalists.

**Figure 5.2** How Buyers Find Visible Experts

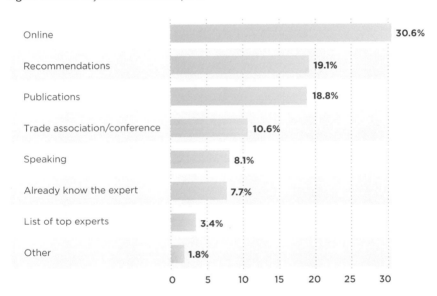

| | |
|---|---|
| Online | 30.6% |
| Recommendations | 19.1% |
| Publications | 18.8% |
| Trade association/conference | 10.6% |
| Speaking | 8.1% |
| Already know the expert | 7.7% |
| List of top experts | 3.4% |
| Other | 1.8% |

While there is nothing revolutionary about the way that clients search for Visible Experts, the study did reveal two important findings:

1. **Buyers search for Visible Experts in multiple ways.** Most buyers use almost five different search methods to look for a Visible Expert. That means a Visible Expert must be visible across multiple channels.

Going online is by far the most popular way for buyers to find Visible Experts.

51

2. **Going online is the most popular way for buyers to find Visible Experts.** Our study was unequivocal—buyers rely on the Internet to locate the high profile experts they hire. Word-of-mouth recommendations and publications tied for a distant second place.

When looking for Visible Experts, search engines, webinars, and LinkedIn account for 70% of all online methods.

When we realized that the Internet was so critical to the search process, we wanted to know more about buyers' online activities. Where do buyers conduct their online research? How do they find answers about Visible Experts? Figure 5.3 breaks out the online search techniques used by our respondents:

**Figure 5.3** Online Techniques Used by Buyers

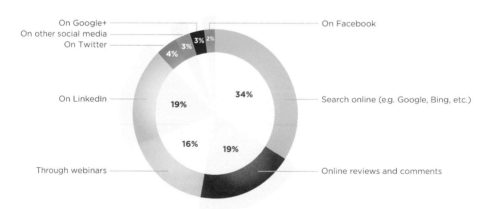

Once again, buyers demonstrated that they use a variety of methods to search for and research Visible Experts—this time, online. Purchasers especially relied on search engines, webinars, and LinkedIn, which together accounted for almost 70% of the online methods used to search for Visible Experts.

Alan Weiss, CEO of Summit Consulting and internationally renowned author and speaker, offers this advice to aspiring Visible Experts: "To establish credibility, you have to spread your message. Try to appear in as many channels as you can—it's great publicity. I never know what will appeal to different people, so I use multiple tools to spread the word: video, blogs, FAQs, books, white papers, and webinars."

## Buyers Evaluate Visible Experts in New Ways

After a buyer has selected a Visible Expert, the last step is performing due diligence. Before they hire an expert, most companies check them out. We wanted to know how buyers performed this final evaluation, so we asked them. Figure 5.4 summarizes their responses.

**Figure 5.4** How Buyers "Check Out" Professional Services Providers

| Category | Percentage |
|---|---|
| Look at their website | 80.8% |
| Search online (e.g. "Google" them) | 63.2% |
| Ask friends or colleagues if they've heard of the person or firm | 62.4% |
| Social media | 59.9% |
| Talk to a reference that they provided | 55.5% |
| I don't check them out | 0.7% |

It turns out that buyers are not only finding providers in multiple ways, but also doing their homework by checking them out in multiple ways.

Fully 80% of participants said that they visit a Visible Expert's website (or the website of their firm) before buying a service. It might be time to reassess your website. When prospects are browsing your website looking for service offerings, case studies, and thought leadership, what will they find?

**80% of buyers visit a Visible Expert's website before buying a service.**

But an expert's website isn't enough. Buyers are looking for experts in multiple channels. They use Google and social media (especially LinkedIn) to fill in background information on their Visible Experts: online reviews and comments, social media pages, court cases, news articles, and more. Today, it's not enough to be present on these channels. You have to create a positive impression, too.

## Expertise Isn't a Given—Buyers Must be Convinced

At this point, the buyer has done a lot of research and evaluation, and they've narrowed down their choices to a single candidate—the person they believe is best for the job. But how do they know the winner is indeed a Visible Expert? What convinced them?

**A personal recommendation is the single most important indicator of expertise.**

As Figure 5.5 demonstrates, buyers evaluate expertise by examining and filtering data from a variety of sources (on average, buyers consider 4.1 of them). It should come as no surprise that a personal recommendation is the single most important factor that validates a candidate's expertise.

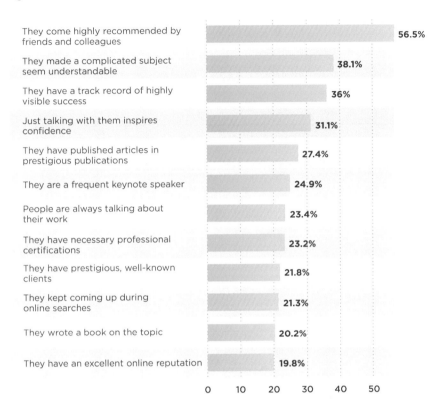

**Figure 5.5** What Convinces Clients that Someone Is a Visible Expert

This makes sense: the better known a Visible Expert, the more people will remember and recommend their name. The more that people recommend their name, the more reliable and prestigious they appear.

The second most-cited factor, however, came as a bit of a surprise. It is not awards, publications, or professional certifications. Instead, it is an expert's ability to explain complicated topics in clear and simple language.

Simplifying the complex may seem counterintuitive to professionals who feel like they need to justify their fees by embracing difficult ideas. But this point lines up neatly with what Visible Experts told us themselves. When asked which factors were most important to career development, Visible Experts put speaking and writing ability at the top of the list, second only to passion and enthusiasm.

For buyers, a provider's ability to explain complicated topics is a clear indicator of expertise.

Jim Collins, author, speaker, and Visible Expert for the Management Consulting world, uses his Hedgehog Concept to explain this phenomenon: "An ancient Greek parable distinguishes between foxes, which know many small things, and hedgehogs, which know one big thing. All good-to-great leaders, it turns out, are hedgehogs. They know how to simplify a complex world into a single, organizing idea—the kind of basic principle that unifies, organizes, and guides all decisions. That's not to say hedgehogs are simplistic. Like great thinkers, who take complexities and boil them down into simple, yet profound, ideas (Adam Smith and the invisible hand, Darwin and evolution), leaders of good-to-great companies develop a Hedgehog Concept that is simple but that reflects penetrating insight and deep understanding."

Jay Baer, President and founder of Convince and Convert, explains it in a different way: "I have a knack for translation. I am not the person who is going to break all new ground. But I'm good at taking a lot of concepts and fast-moving circumstances, identifying patterns, and explaining it in ways that everyone can understand. And everything our company does revolves around that premise."

Bottom line? Great communication skills are a formidable asset.

# Staci Riordan

Staci Riordan, attorney and creator of the fashion law sector, was also an early adopter of content marketing, which she credits with helping her build her book of clients much faster than relying on traditional marketing channels. Using her professional blog, designed and managed by LexBlog, Staci writes weekly articles, and she posts frequently on social channels such as Twitter, where she has over 2,000 followers.

After law school, Staci was hired by the law firm Thelen, LLP, where she launched a fashion law practice group—the first in the country. When Thelen folded in 2008, Staci moved to Fox Rothschild, bringing her fashion clients with her and founding the firm's Fashion Law Practice Group. A little more than seven years after becoming a member of the bar, Fox promoted Staci to equity partner—a rare occurrence in today's market.

Staci believes that the world of legal services is undergoing a major shift. "Times have changed," she notes. "No one does anything the way their parents did. So why would you continue providing legal services the old way?" Today, "being a good lawyer is not enough. Lawyers need to be entrepreneurs. As the way people buy professional services shift, you have to shift too."

For Staci, that shift has meant meeting her clients where they are, and using technology—including SMS, social media channels, and the legal blogging tools provided by Lexblog—to connect with them in new ways. "My clients want to text me, not call me," she says. "And if you're not meeting clients where they are, then how can they find you?"

## Clients Enjoy Multiple Benefits from Hiring a Visible Expert

Finally, we wanted to know whether hiring a Visible Expert was worth it. Did it provide real value? The answer couldn't be clearer. Visible Experts bring more to the table than expected. And the biggest benefit was something of a surprise.

Most clients have a very positive experience working with Visible Experts. And they cite a wide range of benefits—an average of 4.6 per respondent—that spring from such a relationship. But here's where it gets interesting. While problem solving was the most common reason that buyers hired a Visible Expert, that was not the benefit they extolled in the end.

Instead, buyers rank *new learning* as their biggest payoff. Initially, clients don't seek out Visible Experts because they want to be educated. But in retrospect, they identify learning as a top benefit of the engagement. For these clients, working with a Visible Expert not only solved their problem, but also helped them see their path forward more clearly.

**Figure 5.6** Benefits of Working with a Visible Expert

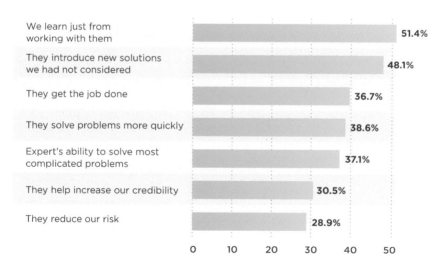

We learn just from working with them — **51.4%**

They introduce new solutions we had not considered — **48.1%**

They get the job done — **36.7%**

They solve problems more quickly — **38.6%**

Expert's ability to solve most complicated problems — **37.1%**

They help increase our credibility — **30.5%**

They reduce our risk — **28.9%**

0  10  20  30  40  50

## Becoming a Visible Expert

In Chapter 4, we learned that there are multiple advantages to becoming a Visible Expert, or having one in your firm. And now we've seen that there are clear benefits for your clients, as well.

So how do you become more visible? The good news is that you don't have to figure it out on your own. There is a replicable, systematic process to becoming a Visible Expert. And in Section 2, we'll teach you how.

In the end, buyers appreciate Visible Experts who educate them.

## TAKEAWAYS

- Clients seek out Visible Experts for one or more of the following reasons:

  * Solving a critical problem

  * Building the brand and winning new business

  * The confidence conferred by an expert

  * To help with a legal proceeding

- Buyers search for Visible Experts in multiple ways, with online search ranked highest.

- Search engines, webinars, and LinkedIn account for almost 70% of the online methods used to search for Visible Experts.

- To confirm a candidate's expertise, a personal recommendation is the single most important factor for buyers, while a Visible Expert's ability to explain complicated topics was ranked second.

- After the fact, buyers identify learning as a top benefit of the Visible Expert engagement. For these clients, working with a Visible Expert not only solved their problem, but also helped them see their path forward more clearly.

# Andrew J. Sherman

Andrew Sherman has done it all: started a business, earned a law degree, become a legend in the field of corporate law, written 26 books, been hired as partner at the global law firm Jones Day, and taught at Georgetown Law School and the University of Maryland's Smith School of Business. Many people might consider Andrew's career history to be quite varied. But Andrew doesn't see it that way.

According to Andrew, "Everything I do is an integrated attempt to maintain reputation as a thought leader and because it adds value to my clients." His ability to participate in such a wide range of professional and content marketing activities was key to helping Andrew become well known, greatly expanding both his sphere of influence and his reputation.

What drives him? "At the end of the day, I really can't imagine doing anything else," he says. "And if you don't feel that commitment, you aren't going to put the time in. I don't think you can rise to the level of Visible Expert without being in love with your work." He offers this advice for those wishing to do the same: "Be passionate about what you do, and don't ever take your position for granted. Keep investing in yourself. And keep creating new tools and resources to keep your status."

The average
Fast Tracker is
more than half
a level ahead
of the average
Visible Expert.

# The Ascent of the Visible Expert

# CHAPTER 6

# Introducing the
# *Fast Trackers*

In section one, we learned that becoming a Visible Expert confers multiple benefits on you, your firm, and your clients. We saw what happens at each stage of a Visible Expert's ascent and how visibility and profitability grow, hand-in-hand. Our next task was to figure out how the process occurred. Which factors were essential to becoming a Visible Expert? If we could answer that question, we would have our brass ring—the ability to replicate the process for others.

The data showed us where to begin. Although the Visible Experts in our study had followed different career paths across a variety of industries, they shared certain fundamental tools, activities, and skillsets. In our analysis, we found that the order of these elements did not matter—some of them could be completed simultaneously, while others could be added along the way. In this sense they were more like ingredients or building blocks than steps. These building blocks would form the foundation of our Visible Expert strategy.

> Visible Experts use the same tools, activities, and skillsets to reach the top.

But as we crunched the numbers, something even more interesting became apparent. Not only was the process replicable, but there was also a way to get there *faster*. There appeared to be a fast track to becoming a Visible Expert, and some of our study participants had figured out how to get on it. Just how much faster were these Fast Trackers rising? And were they benefiting in other areas? Our research was about to show us.

> We discovered a *fast track* to becoming a Visible Expert.

Tired of a life of constant business travel and wanting more time with his young family, Visible Expert Ian Brodie left the world of corporate consulting in 2007 to start consulting as a solo practitioner. Now he helps consultants and coaches in the professional services industry attract new clients and grow their businesses. In six short years he has become a true Visible Expert in his field, building a successful business branded around his own name, becoming known as a marketing guru throughout the UK and US, and substantially increasing his earning power. His fees have risen 80-90% over the past three years.

# A Shortcut to Success

According to an old business adage, there's no shortcut to success. While we haven't discovered a way around hard work, our Fast Trackers showed us a shorter path to becoming a Visible Expert.

Most Visible Experts remain at each level of visibility for almost five years, but our Fast Trackers spent just 10 months at a level before moving up to the next.

*Fast Trackers* rise to the top 5X faster than other Visible Experts.

As you can see in Figure 6.1, Fast Trackers have discovered a faster and more efficient way to become a Visible Expert. Yes, a shortcut to success.

**Figure 6.1** Average Speed of Ascent, Fast Trackers vs. Visible Experts

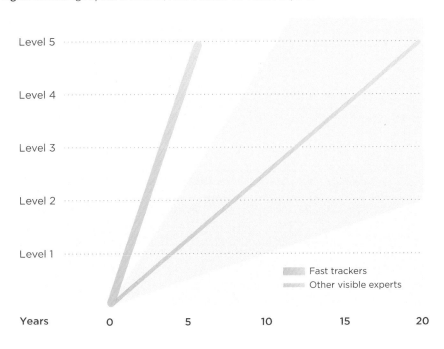

Fast trackers
Other visible experts

But Fast Trackers have more than just speed going for them—we uncovered a host of other benefits, too. In fact, Fast Trackers outpace the other Visible Experts in every category. In an already elite group, Fast Trackers are the cream of the Visible Expert crop. Let's take a look at the findings.

*Fast Trackers outpace other Visible Experts in every category.*

## Going Faster and Farther

Besides getting there faster, Fast Trackers are also going farther. In fact, at any given point the average Fast Tracker is more than half a level ahead of the average Visible Expert.

Fast Trackers also have greater online visibility. Using a popular domain authority tool available through Moz.com, we learned that the average online authority of a Fast Tracker's website is over 10 points higher than that of other Visible Experts (Moz uses a 0-100 logarithmic scale to indicate the potential of a website to rank well in search engines).

The average Fast Tracker is more than half a level ahead of the average Visible Expert.

## Fast Trackers Have the Edge

The trend continues across all of the business metrics we measured. Fast Trackers were beating their peers in content output, speaking and partnership inquiries, and generating inbound leads. Their audiences tended to be better acquainted with their specialty, and they were able to be more selective in their clients.

Some of the Fast Trackers' gains were modest. For instance, we found that Fast Trackers are only slightly more likely to attract partnership inquiries and inbound leads. But some differences were significant. For example, Fast Trackers were three times more likely than the average Visible Expert to charge higher fees. Taken as an aggregate, these wins over the competition—both small and large—add up to a powerful marketplace advantage.

> Fast Trackers are 3X more likely to charge higher rates.

**Figure 6.2** The Fast Track Advantage

Compared to all other Visible Experts, Fast Trackers are:

- 4.5X more likely to receive speaking inquiries
- 3X more likely to charge higher rates
- 2X more likely to attract an audience that is already educated
- 1.4X more likely to attract more inbound leads
- 1.3X more likely to achieve more partnership opportunities

## The Secret of the Fast Track

Once we discovered there was a faster and even more advantageous way to get to the top, we had to know more. What were the Fast Trackers doing differently? When we compared the actions of the Fast Trackers against those of the other Visible Experts, we had our answer. We found that the Fast Trackers were doing all of the things that the others were doing—and more.

In the following chapters we'll lay out a plan to become a Visible Expert, including the secret ingredients that set Fast Trackers apart from the rest.

### TAKEAWAYS

- Although Visible Experts follow different career paths, they all rely on the same tools, activities, and skillsets to get to the top.

- Some Visible Experts get to the top faster. We call these experts Fast Trackers.

- Fast Trackers rise to the top 5X faster than other Visible Experts.

- Fast Trackers outpace other Visible Experts in every category: website authority, content output, speaking and partnership inquiries, generating inbound leads, and commanding premium fees.

# Lori Randall Stradtman

Lori Randall Stradtman didn't set out
to become a Visible Expert. When this
divorced mom returned to college for
a second degree in communications,
she was thinking only of how to
support her three kids. Fast forward
eight years, and Lori is an author, a
public speaker, and an in-demand
social media strategist who runs her
own company.

For Lori, blogging was the key to
success. After graduation, Lori started a blog on social media and
marketing and landed a marketing director job. But her blog was
gaining a lot of attention, and she saw that social media could be
used to share ideas and generate buzz—something her firm was
not doing.

So Lori started her own web design company using a brand-new
social-media-based business model and offering a brand-new
social media service. Her first client was located in Dubai. Her
second was in Silicon Valley. She thought, "Why splash around in
a small pool when you can make a bigger impact?"

Lori's visibility exploded in 2011, when the publishing giant Wiley
invited her to write a book in their famous *Dummies* series. The
book, *Online Reputation Management for Dummies*, became
Amazon's second best-selling book in the Public Relations
category within a month of publication.

Giving—the underlying principle of content marketing—is the
philosophy behind Lori's entire career. She was so motivated by
the idea of giving that she created a scalable system for doing so,
making it a focal point in her book. "I want to see organizations
putting good and genuinely helpful stuff out into the world," she
says. "It's as simple as that."

# CHAPTER 7:

# Components of a Visible Expert Brand

Once we understood what our research was telling us, our next move was clear: to develop a program that any qualified person could follow to become a Visible Expert. But we soon realized that becoming a Visible Expert is not a step-by-step process. In fact, it's made up of seven components, and they don't have to occur in any specific order.

Like building blocks, these components are connected and interdependent—as you rise through the levels of visibility you'll need to address all of them. In this chapter we will examine these seven building blocks, along with the extra features that allow Fast Trackers to rise faster than the rest.

Visible Experts rely on 7 essential building blocks. They don't need to occur in a particular order.

## The Seven Building Blocks

### 1. Commit to Becoming a Visible Expert
You don't become an industry expert by accident: This is true of all great achievements. Winning an Olympic medal starts

with a vision and takes years of training to achieve success. Becoming a Visible Expert is no different. It takes diligence—and a great deal of strategy, planning, and scheduling.

Many of the Visible Experts in our study told us their biggest regret was not becoming more deliberate and strategic earlier in their career. They emphasized the importance of commitment—making sure you know what you want, then being passionate and authentic and working hard.

Becoming a Visible Expert requires planning, strategy, and scheduling.

"At the end of the day, I really can't imagine doing anything else," says Andrew Sherman, a professor, highly sought corporate law attorney, senior partner at Jones Day, and author of 26 books. "If you don't feel that commitment, you aren't going to put the time in. I don't think you can rise to the level of Visible Expert without being in love with your work." His advice? "Be passionate about what you do, and don't ever take your position for granted."

So first decide if you really want to become a Visible Expert. Then put the necessary level of commitment behind it.

**2. Develop a Strategy for your Visible Expert Brand**
We define your brand as the product of your reputation and your visibility. To become a Visible Expert, you must develop both. You'll need to be strategic about branding yourself, being careful to communicate a consistent message across all of your channels. In order to build visibility—to many people, the most challenging part of becoming a Visible Expert—you'll need to develop a strong offline and online presence. We will talk in detail about building visibility a little later in this chapter.

"You don't wake up one day and say 'I'm a Visible Expert,' just as you wouldn't wake up and say 'I'm going to win a gold medal today.' It takes lots of training. You need to work to establish and maintain a reputation. Americans have short memories, and thought leadership is about sustaining that commitment to being the best, to keeping your reputation at the top."

   **– Andrew Sherman,** corporate law attorney, professor, and author of 26 books

It's important to understand that an expert's brand need not compete against the brand of his or her firm. In fact, the two brands should complement one another.

### 3. Build Visibility in a Target Market

You could be the most talented expert in the world, but without an audience, you will toil in obscurity. The difference between Visible Experts and other professionals is that Visible Experts are well known to their target audience.

Visible Experts achieve high visibility in a number of ways: by building a significant online presence, by networking and forging partnerships, and by seizing opportunity and taking appropriate entrepreneurial risks.

In contrast to other professionals, Visible Experts are well known within a targeted audience.

The mistake that many professionals make, says Visible Expert Ian Brodie, is that "most shy away from publishing anything—blogs, videos, articles, etc. So they're only sharing one on one with their clients, and they grow slowly. The fastest way to make an impact is to get your information visible to as many people as possible." Ian's go-to content marketing channels include his blog, email newsletters, webinars, and Twitter, on which he has attracted over 99,000 followers.

To build their own expertise, Visible Experts also tend to align themselves with other Visible Experts, keeping abreast of their innovations and partnering whenever it makes strategic sense. In this way, you can benefit from their visibility and reputation.

Successful Visible Experts also make sure that their expertise indicators are visible. As they engage in expertise-building activities, they are careful to promote and advertise these pursuits, gaining double mileage from them. For example, if they attend an industry conference to learn more about a specific topic, they are also tweeting or blogging about the experience.

### 4. Strengthen your Expertise

If you don't have expertise, you can't be a Visible Expert. Sorry. All of the visibility in the world won't save you, and clients will quickly see through the hype.

To build expertise, study participants put a high premium on continuously improving their skills and educating themselves. This resolve kept them on the cutting edge, and it translated into business success for their clients as they applied new techniques and innovations to their clients' problems.

If you don't have expertise, you can't be a Visible Expert.

Visible Experts also reported the importance of asking questions and never overestimating their abilities. The very best have learned to keep their egos in check as they rise through the levels.

### 5. Refine your Communication Skills

An expert's ability to communicate lies at the foundation of the soft skillset we mentioned earlier. Most Visible Experts shine in this area — they are equally comfortable leading a webinar, delivering a keynote, or allaying a client's worries in a conference room.

# Rick Telberg

Already a pioneer of digital publishing when the Internet boom hit in the early 2000s, Rick Telberg became one of the first to harness online media and marketing for the accounting and finance industry. In 2001, he was recruited by the American Institute of Certified Public Accountants (AICPA), where he launched an online publishing operation that grew to a circulation of over 1 million. This initiative included innovative social media, digital marketing, and online publishing strategies.

By 2004, Rick had founded his own consulting business, Bay Street Group, LLC, which helped accounting firms and vendors leverage their intellectual assets and develop new business opportunities and revenue streams. CPA2Biz, AICPA, IBM, Hewlett-Packard, and Blackberry were among his earliest clients.

Rick quickly realized that Bay Street Group would benefit from a media wing to promote its research findings and analysis. So he launched CPA Trendlines, which delivers trends and industry news to the tax, accounting, and finance industry.

Rick believes that specialization allowed his media group to emerge as an industry powerhouse. With a background in both print and online journalism and a deep insight into the accounting and finance world, he was the perfect person to capitalize on the digital media revolution. And while other firms faltered during the banking crisis of 2007, Rick seized the opportunity to differentiate. "Professionals needed real-time business information to respond to their fast-changing world," he says, "and we were able to fill that need." Rick saw a gap that no one else was filling, and he quickly addressed the demand.

But not everyone is a naturally gifted public speaker or writer. If you have identified communication as an area of weakness, now is the time to tackle this challenge head-on. These are skills you can master with some expert coaching.

As Chris Mercer of Mercer Capital says, "Business development is an attitude, and you have to wake up every morning doing it. You need to write, speak, and make yourself known. I recognized that if I didn't take myself outbound, my business wouldn't succeed. Initially, that was hard for me. At heart, I have an introverted personality, but the desire not to fail was a motivator!"

> Visible Experts must be good communicators.

You can overcome your weaknesses, too. First you need to recognize where they lie.

### 6. Become a Teacher

One of the defining characteristics of a Visible Expert is their ability to make complicated subjects understandable and reassure clients that their problems will be resolved. In our study, both buyers and Visible Experts reported that this soft skillset was vital—and one of the major differences that sets Visible Experts apart from other professionals.

"An important thing I learned is to be a translator between my professional language and the way that most people perceive something," says architect Sarah Susanka. "Many architects are talking in a language that normal people do not comprehend. So I pride myself in being able to look at a far-out, avant-garde building and help regular people understand it. I guess I enjoy putting my work into language that is accessible to regular people."

> Visible Experts make complicated subjects easy to understand.

The truth is that the best Visible Experts are also great teachers. They are motivators, excited about their industry niche, and they inspire the people around them. Above all, they engage and educate their audiences, imparting practical wisdom.

## 7. Get the Help You Need

It's probably hard for you to imagine how someone can acquire all the skills and knowledge they need to become an accomplished Visible Expert. The level of time commitment required is significant. For instance, you may recognize that your writing or speaking skills aren't up to snuff. Or you may feel at a loss when it comes to planning your strategy. When you think about all the specialized skills you'll need to build your expert brand, from search engine optimization to public relations, it's easy to get discouraged. And you would be right: it's not a cakewalk.

In fact, most Visible Experts seek out help at some point during the process. As you ascend in visibility, experiencing both increased fees and reduced time, getting help often means hiring. Management consulting guru Jim Collins understands the importance of surrounding yourself with great people. In his book, *Good to Great and the Social Sectors*, Jim says that the great leaders and companies are the ones "focused on getting and hanging on to the right people in the first place—those who are productively neurotic, those who are self-motivated and self-disciplined, those who wake up every day, compulsively driven to do the best they can because it is simply part of their DNA... Lack of resources is no excuse for lack of rigor—it makes selectivity all the more vital." This story was repeated by many of the Visible Experts in our study, who said that they could not do it without the support of a great

> In contrast to other professionals, Visible Experts are well known within a targeted audience.

team. So don't be afraid to seek out help where and when you need it.

None of these activities is a one-and-done enterprise. They have to be sustained over time. Even Level 5 Visible Experts continue to engage in outreach when it fits their strategy.

## The Fast Track

In our research, we found that Fast Trackers employ all of the same components as other Visible Experts—except they add three more. And those extra features make a huge difference, allowing them to rise five times faster than their Visible Expert peers. Read on to discover their secrets.

Fast Trackers do these three things differently.

### Fast Track Secret 1: Focus on a Target Market
Fast Trackers taught us that finding a niche or focusing on a very specific audience helps experts become famous faster.

Compared to other Visible Experts, Fast Trackers were more than twice as likely to focus their expertise on a narrow target market, and to do so earlier in their careers. This makes it easier to differentiate themselves from competitors, which also makes branding and marketing easier. Fast Trackers also seek out strategic partnerships that closely align with their specialty.

In a recent TED talk, Visible Expert Seth Godin, the international author, speaker, and digital marketing innovator described the power of focus. "The idea you create, the product you create—it's not for everyone. It's not a mass thing. That's not what this is about. What it's about instead is finding the true believers."

Finding a niche helps experts become famous faster.

These "true believers" will then become your advocates and grow your brand for you. Focus also gives you an angle to challenge conventional thinking and established methods. True thought leaders often hold strong opinions and take unexpected positions. Having narrow expertise provides a platform to promote your ideas.

## Fast Track Secret 2: Embrace Content Marketing

While all Visible Experts use quality content to build their brands, Fast Trackers have a powerful content marketing strategy in place. These fast risers start sooner, producing more content, more frequently, and on more channels.

**Figure 7.1** Fast Trackers Use Content Marketing Earlier and More Strategically, When Compared to all Other Visible Experts.

- 4X more likely to blog and podcast earlier in their careers

- 2X more likely to create valuable content on a regular basis

- 1.9X more likely to use content to drive leads

Staci Riordan, attorney and creator of the fashion law sector, was also an early adopter of content marketing, which she credits with helping her build her book of clients much faster than relying on traditional marketing channels. Using technical and marketing tools provided by LexBlog, Staci writes weekly articles for her professional blog, and she posts frequently on social channels such as Twitter, where she has over 2,000 followers. She also delivers keynotes or speeches for at least one industry event per month. At the end of the day, Staci says, "people want to work with people they like— someone who resonates with them. And because of blogging, social media, and public speaking, people feel like they know me although they've never met me."

Fast Trackers rely on content marketing.

We discuss content marketing further in the next chapter, where you'll learn about its crucial role in promoting expertise.

### Fast Track Secret 3: Write a Book

Almost 85% of Fast Trackers have written a strategically focused book. Again and again, our top-level Visible Experts reported that a book is a visibility catalyst, conferring instant credibility and opening doors to elite speaking engagements and partnerships such as TED talks, media interviews, and top industry conference keynotes.

"My book was a force multiplier," says Visible Expert Tim Ash, CEO of Site Tuners. "I could have gotten there without it, but it would have been a lot harder. It's an expensive and painful investment, but so worth it! It is the best $12 business card I've ever had—there's nothing like getting a signed copy of a book from the author to help advance the sale."

85% of Fast Trackers have written a book.

Does it have to be a book? Not necessarily. There are other signature pieces that convey expertise and increase visibility. For example, an expert could publish a specialty blog that is required reading in your clients' industry. But in most cases, a highly focused book is the quickest and surest path to Visible Expert status.

## Building Your Tower

Becoming a Visible Expert is like building a tower: You must be careful and strategic as you go, recognizing that each block is dependent on those around it. Neglect a certain block, or move carelessly, and the whole tower can fall.

Now that we've explored each individual building block, it's time to start building. Chapter 8 will take you through the tools you'll need to build your visibility, while Chapter 9 will lay out the blueprint, teaching you how to develop a Visible Expert program for you or your firm. *Grab your hardhat and get ready to break some new ground.*

## TAKEAWAYS

- Most Visible Experts employ these 7 essential building blocks:
    - \* Commit to becoming a Visible Expert
    - \* Develop a strategy for your Visible Expert brand
    - \* Build visibility in a target market
    - \* Strengthen your expertise
    - \* Refine your communication skills
    - \* Become a teacher
    - \* Get the help you need
- Fast Trackers add 3 extra components:
    - \* Focus on a niche
    - \* Embrace content marketing
    - \* Write a book

# Alan Weiss

In 1986, Alan Weiss set up shop as a solo consultant focusing on organizational development. Four years later, he had grown his practice into a million-dollar business with a client list of Fortune 1000 companies, including Merck, Hewlett-Packard, GE, Mercedes-Benz, and The New York Times Corporation. Today, he is a highly sought public speaker, author, and consultant to consultants.

Early on, Alan decided he would write books to boost his visibility. In 1992, after being rejected by 16 publishers, Alan hit a bulls-eye when McGraw-Hill published his third book, *Million Dollar Consulting*. The book—now in its fourth printing—was a runaway hit, propelling Alan's emergence as a Visible Expert. Today, Alan has written 55 books that have been translated into 12 languages.

Consultants are often reluctant to give anything away for free, but Alan discovered that giving away intellectual property was key to growing his brand. Alan believes that giving away information expands your reputation and visibility, making your paid services more valuable. He says, "Someone will read your book and then they will want to pay more to talk to the real person."

Specialization also helped Alan grow his visibility, and his specialization changed over time. Early on, Alan targeted Fortune 1000 companies. Today, he focuses on the "retail consumer"— consultants who want to emulate his model. Alan found that carefully choosing his audience and focusing his message on topics of interest to that audience made it easier to differentiate and become recognized. Moral of the story? If you want to be a Visible Expert, it's easier to be a big fish in a small pond. Just choose your pond carefully.

# CHAPTER 8

# The Visibility Toolkit

In the last chapter, we explored the building blocks required to become a Visible Expert, along with the extra components that accelerate the Fast Trackers' ascent. In this chapter, we'll look at the tools and techniques that Visible Experts use to become more visible to their target audience. These are the tools you will use to build your *expert brand*.

## Lead Sources

To figure out which tools are the most effective, we needed to start at the end and consider every firm's ultimate objective: to attract new business. So we asked our Visible Experts to list their top lead sources. Figure 8.1 displays the top ten. It's important to note that most Visible Experts mentioned multiple lead sources.

Visible Experts generate leads from a wide range of sources.

**Figure 8.1** Visible Experts' Top 10 Lead Sources

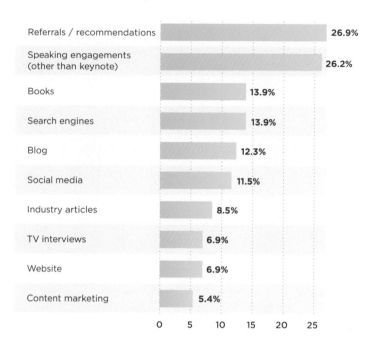

Clearly, Visible Experts generate leads from a wide range of sources, including referrals, speaking engagements, search engines, books, and blogs. It should come as no surprise that referrals and recommendations top the chart. As we described in our book *Inside the Buyer's Brain*, referrals continue to be a powerful way to generate leads. The reason? Buyers trust friends, colleagues, and business partners to steer them in the right direction.

Visible Experts generate leads from a wide range of sources.

A bigger surprise is that speaking engagements are a close second. Why are these events such a powerful lead generator? We have a theory. Rather than educating people one-on-one, speaking engagements allow Visible Experts to educate and inspire an entire room full of people—a focused audience that has invested time and money to learn about a specific subject. This activity becomes even more powerful as experts move up in the ranks, taking on more important speaking roles at top industry conferences.

Staci Riordan, creator of the fashion law sector and a partner at the law firm Fox Rothschild, explains how it works: "Public speaking helps me be perceived as an expert and brings in a lot of new leads. It builds credibility and helps people become aware of what you specialize in. I do at least one speaking engagement a month. At this point, events seek me out. I have to be choosy, and I say 'no' a lot."

> Speaking engagements are powerful lead generators.

## The Power of SEO

Search engines are also strong lead generators, ranking above all other online activities. This makes sense: If you invest in search engine optimization (SEO), all of your other tools and techniques become more effective.

In a nutshell, SEO is a set of activities that help search engines such as Google, Yahoo, and Bing find and rank your website, blog posts, or any of your other online content. In the competitive online environment, SEO-optimized content has a much better chance of being discovered by prospects searching online for information or help. You can post a panoply of wonderful articles, books, and blog posts to your website—but without SEO, they aren't likely to be found. For experts who want to become more visible and generate leads online, this is a critical technique.

> For driving leads, search engines out-rank all other online activities.

Marketing consultant Ian Brodie relies on SEO to grow his firm. "When you're small, you have to knock on some doors," he told us. "But as I became more visible, people started to reach out to me, instead." Today, more and more of his new leads come to him "pre-qualified," finding him through referrals or through his valuable content, which he optimizes for SEO and provides for free on his website. "I don't do any other business development, and no networking. People find me through my blog and social media."

## Tools and Techniques

Once we had explored lead sources, we went back to the beginning and asked which tools Visible Experts use on a daily basis. We found that experts employ a wide range of tools to build visibility and drive leads. In fact, the average Visible Expert in our study used about 16 different tools! The chart below lists the top ten.

**Figure 8.2** Popularity of Tools (Percent of Visible Experts Who Use Each Tool)

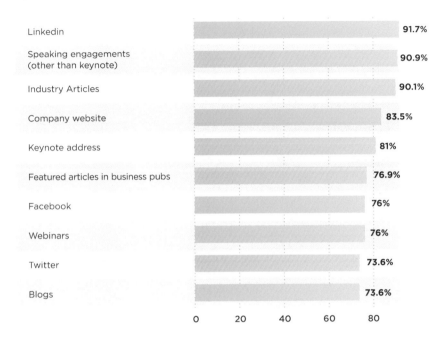

| Tool | Percent |
|---|---|
| Linkedin | 91.7% |
| Speaking engagements (other than keynote) | 90.9% |
| Industry Articles | 90.1% |
| Company website | 83.5% |
| Keynote address | 81% |
| Featured articles in business pubs | 76.9% |
| Facebook | 76% |
| Webinars | 76% |
| Twitter | 73.6% |
| Blogs | 73.6% |

As we looked at this data, we made a few observations. As the top social network for professionals, LinkedIn ranks as the most popular tool. Once again, speaking engagements run a close second. And keynote addresses are important enough that they warrant their own special category, apart from other speaking engagements.

This chart also speaks to the importance of content marketing. Unlike conventional marketing that pushes your message out to your audience, content marketing focuses on creating and disseminating free, valuable

*Visible Experts' most popular tools are also content marketing tools.*

content that attracts interested parties to you like a magnet. Is it a coincidence that all ten of the Visible Experts' most popular tools are also content marketing tools? We don't think so.

Next, we wanted to know which of these tools and techniques had the greatest total impact. The results are shown in Figure 8.3. Notice that this chart is quite similar to the lead source chart from Figure 8.1—the tools that have the biggest impact also tend to generate the most leads.

**Figure 8.3** Total Impact of Tools

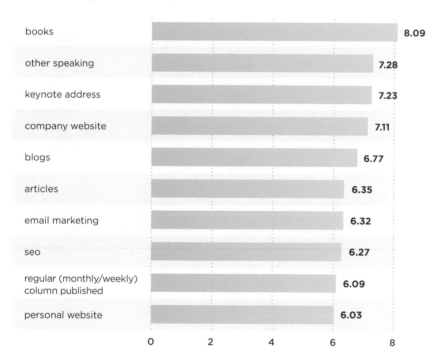

Speaking engagements continue to show their power, placing second and third on the list of most impactful tools. It is interesting to note that quite a few of the most popular tools are not ranked as highly effective, and vice versa. For example, SEO and personal websites demonstrate a high level of impact, yet they do not appear in the top ten most popular tools. We see the opposite trend with social channels like LinkedIn, Facebook, and Twitter. These social tools have high popularity but relatively lower impact, when taken on their own. But this does not mean that you should ignore social media. To understand why, let's consider the example of another ubiquitous tool: your email address.

For Visible Experts, the effect of appearing in multiple places boosts overall visibility.

A professional email address is not likely to generate leads for you, but we all know it's an essential tool. Without one, you would be neither accessible nor credible. Your social profiles offer similar benefits. While not producing the highest overall impact, these profiles allow you to be found online, present your credentials, and give prospects a way to contact you. Today, they too are special tools. Remember that most Visible Experts use a wide variety of tools, allowing them to appear in multiple places. That gives them greater overall visibility and accessibility.

But there is one crucial bit of evidence in this data we haven't discussed: *books*. Books have the highest impact of all, yet their usage is so low that they don't even appear in the list of top ten most popular tools. What's going on here?

For building visibility, books deliver the highest impact.

In chapter 7, we learned that Fast Trackers rely on books to boost their visibility, so it makes a lot of sense that the data shows books delivering the highest overall impact. However, books are difficult to produce, so most Visible Experts never tackle them. But the Fast Trackers do. And if *you* want to rise through the ranks faster, you should, too.

Listen to Visible Expert Chris Mercer, of Mercer Capital: "Books have been absolutely essential in creating the credibility that we market in, under, and around. I published my first book, *Valuing Financial Institutions*, in 1992. The book put me into a rare group of a half-dozen people who had written anything about valuation. It established me as an expert in the valuation niche."

Chris Mercer is not alone—earlier in this book, Tim Ash, Lori Randall Stradtman, and Sarah Susanka spoke about how important books were to increasing their visibility, and this experience has been repeated by almost all of the high-level Visible Experts in our study.

## ROE: The Best of the Best Tools

Finally, we looked at the effort that Visible Experts put into tools and techniques, measuring effort against impact to determine the return on effort (ROE) for each tool. This yielded a best of the best, the top five tools that give you the most bang for your time.

**The winners were:**

1. Books

2. Online video

3. Blog posts

4. News articles that feature the Visible Expert

5. Keynote addresses

All five of these can be classified as content marketing techniques. And books come out on top with a powerful return on effort. Content marketing—and books in particular—contribute heavily to Fast Trackers' success.

There are also a few surprises on this list of winners. Online video makes its first appearance. This educational approach is growing in popularity, with technology making it easier and less expensive to produce. And featured news articles sneak into the top five, showing the power of the media to expand both visibility and authority.

## Developing a Plan

At this point, you've learned which components you'll need to become a Visible Expert, as well as which tools should be in your toolkit. You're almost ready to begin your ascent. In the next chapter, we will lay out a Visible Expert program, a step-by-step plan to get you to the top.

## TAKEAWAYS

- Visible Experts generate leads from a range of sources, with referrals, speaking engagements, and search engines providing the most activity.

- All of the Visible Experts' ten most popular tools are content marketing techniques. When you create free, valuable content, you build your brand.

- Visible Experts use a wide variety of tools, allowing them to appear in multiple places—which boosts their visibility and accessibility.

- Five tools offer the greatest return on effort:

  * Books

  * Online video

  * Blog posts

  * News articles that feature the Visible Expert

  * Keynote addresses

# Warren Buffett

Investment wizard Warren Buffett was an entrepreneur from the very start. As a boy, he invested money from soft drink sales and a paper route into 40 acres of land, which he then leased for a comfortable margin—not bad for a 14-year-old!

While honing his craft at Columbia Business School in 1951, his advisor— the lauded "Father of Value Investing," Benjamin Graham—discouraged him from pursuing a career on Wall Street. And when Graham caved and offered him a position, the young Warren expanded upon his mentor's investment strategy, introducing a brand new practice to the industry. Instead of looking only at a stock's dollar value, Warren began examining the whole company behind the stock, accounting for management style and competitive advantage in his analysis. Needless to say, this approach paid off.

Despite being ranked the wealthiest person in the world in 2008, Warren continues to live a humble and frugal life. Rumored to carry neither a cell phone nor a personal computer, he lives in the same Omaha residence he bought for $31,500 in 1958. He has also pledged to disperse 99% of his fortune to charity and has already given the largest donation in history—approximately $30.7 billion—to the Bill and Melinda Gates Foundation.

Now in his mid-eighties, Warren remains CEO of Berkshire Hathaway. A life-long learner, he reads five newspapers a day. His reputation has expanded far beyond the finance world, and he has become known world-wide for his philanthropic and political efforts, including serving as an advisor for the Nuclear Threat Initiative. A value investor by trade and a philanthropist at heart, Warren Buffett is one Global Superstar who has never lost touch with his roots.

# CHAPTER 9:

# The Visible Expert Program

In Chapter 7 we uncovered the components that all Visible Experts must have in place to achieve success, and we learned what Fast Trackers do differently to turbocharge their ascent. In Chapter 8, we explored the tools you will need to begin your journey. But how do you put those components and tools into action? You'll need a plan. And that's the focus of this chapter. Follow these seven steps, and start climbing!

### Step 1: Select the Candidate(s)

To begin, you need to select one or more candidates from your firm. Now, the best Visible Expert candidate isn't always the person with the most experience or seniority in the firm. The ideal candidate will balance practical factors, such as availability and area of expertise, with their *soft skillset* (the ability to work hard, to teach others, and to project confidence even in the face of challenges).

> Candidate selection is the first step of the program.

For the remainder of this chapter, let's assume that you, the reader, are the Visible Expert candidate. Just keep in mind that this program can apply to any candidate, or even a team, in your firm.

Next, assess your current visibility level, as well as your strengths and weaknesses.

### Step 2: Assess Your Status

What is your current status? What level of visibility, if any, have you already achieved? Now is the time to find out. While you'll need to determine your current visibility level, you'll also want to assess your strengths and weaknesses. That's how you'll know where to focus your efforts.

After taking his consulting practice solo in 1986, Visible Expert Alan Weiss is now a recognized authority, earning $3 million a year as an author, a public speaker, and a consultant to consultants. Today, he helps others become successful solo practitioners. Alan believes that every aspiring Visible Expert should undergo a thorough self evaluation. If you take the time to figure out your worth and what makes your value proposition different, you will have the confidence to deliver that message to clients and prospective clients. "At the end of the day," Alan says, "you need to believe: the client chose me because I'm the best at what I do."

During your assessment, you will establish a baseline so that you know where you are today and how far you have to go. An assessment consists of several components:

- *Expertise and Reputation:* What are you known for? What does the marketplace think about you? Consider a variety of expert indicators as you answer these questions, including any books, media mentions, reviews, and references from other people.

- **Visibility:** How well known are you, today? Do you write or speak frequently, and are your materials easy for people to find and access? Are you available in the places where your prospects are looking? How easy are you to find on Google, Bing, and Yahoo?

- **Skill Levels:** As we learned in Chapter 7, every Visible Expert must master a basic set of skills, including public speaking, writing, and the ability to use online tools such as social media and blogging. How would you rank your proficiency with each of these? Where do you need to improve?

- **Business Impact:** What is the impact of your visibility and expertise? How many leads do you generate? Are strategic partners attracted to your firm? Has your expertise enhanced your firm's brand?

- **Foundation:** Do you have the appropriate foundational tools and marketing materials in place? These include a sophisticated website, media kit with headshots and a bio, and other materials and infrastructure you can use to promote your *expert brand.*

### Step 3: Develop a Strategy

Once you have established where you lie on the Visible Expert spectrum, you can start developing your strategy. How? You need to address five key areas:

- **Refine Your Expertise:** Refining your expertise includes establishing your niche, performing a competitive analysis, and creating a positioning statement. Let's look at each of these:

  * *Establish your niche:* What are you known for, and how can you increase your visibility and expertise inside that space? For example, are you an authority in healthcare IT security, or a general IT security expert? Do you want to focus your area of expertise, like the Fast Trackers do? If so, make sure there is a sufficiently large market to support your narrow specialty.

  * *Perform a competitive analysis:* Who are your competitors, and how do you stack up? What are they doing differently, and are those differences positive or negative? How will you differentiate yourself from them?

  * *Create a positioning statement:* Your positioning statement is a short, carefully crafted paragraph that explains the nature and scope of your expertise and positions you relative to other competing experts. It will force you to articulate who you are and how you are different, and it will inspire the messaging you build around your brand.

Your positioning statement positions you relative to other experts.

Visible Expert Jay Baer, CEO and founder of Convince and Convert, uses self-assessment and specialization to make his business more successful. "That old adage that 'any money is good money'—that's not really true. Any time you take your eye off the ball to accept a project that's not getting you ahead, you're diluting yourself and your value. Every year we sit down and look at what we've done. We come up with a list of 15% of activities that didn't get us ahead, and we stop doing them. The trick to running a successful business is to figure out what you are uniquely qualified to do—and then do only that."

- **Define Your Audience:** Whom are you trying to influence? What are their interests? Where do they congregate, both online and offline? Identifying your audience will shape the rest of your strategy. Do you need to find a way to get in front of a certain target group? Do other experts know you? Journalists? Decision makers? You'll also want to generate a list of topics that are of interest to your audience. Later, you will bring your unique viewpoint to these topics in your writing and speaking engagements.

- **Identify Visibility Tools:** The primary goal of a Visible Expert program is to help you become as well known as possible to your target audience. So after you've identified an area of specialty, you'll need a way to promote yourself, to make yourself more visible. To do this, you will take advantage of many of the content marketing and promotional tools we discussed in Chapter 8, such as blogging, speaking engagements, and social media.

> The goal is to become as well known as possible to your target audience.

- **Identify Promotional Channels:** How will you select your channels? Will you have a separate website or blog in addition to your firm's page? Will you host webinars or fly to speaking engagements? The answer is to follow your audience. If your audience is on Facebook, go there. If your audience attends a specific industry conference, offer to make a presentation. Of course, not every method works for every Visible Expert, so you won't need to do them all.

> "I've built a different kind of law practice based on connecting with my clients and going around traditional gatekeepers. You have to meet your clients where they are. I am a fashion lawyer. So I don't go to lawyer events—I go to fashion events. And I do social media, blogging, and speaking at fashion events. We're going to see a shift in law. You can be at forefront, or you can be behind the curve."
>
> — **Staci Riordan,** Visible Expert for the fashion law industry

**Identify Resources:** Visible Experts know they can't do it alone. Do you need help developing certain skills? Creating content? Identify the areas where you can't go it alone, then find the people and resources that can assist you.

> Michael Graves, the internationally renowned architect and designer, realized early on that he could not do it all alone. "I run my own firm, but I'm not a very good administrator," he said in a recent interview. "So early on I hired somebody who could pay the bills, who could make sure we were solvent in terms of our practice. And I was the one who would make the drawings and give the lectures and go to the interviews and try to bring the work home to our office."

# Jim Collins

Management consulting guru Jim Collins was working for Hewlett-Packard as a product manager when he discovered his talent for teaching the complexities of computer networking. But computer networking didn't hold his interest for long—what he really loved was translating complex ideas into easily understood concepts. So Jim left the business world to pursue teaching at Stanford University's Graduate School of Business, where he received the Distinguished Teaching Award in 1992. Today, he runs a management laboratory that he founded himself. He also writes extensively, including contributions to *Harvard Business Review*, *Business Week*, and *Fortune* magazine.

Now Jim is a celebrated author of more than five management books including his global bestseller, *Good to Great*, which sold 2.5 million copies and has been translated into 32 languages. In the book, Jim describes his research into the *Hedgehog Concept*, in which the best business leaders pinpoint their strongest skill, applying it with passion to achieve growth in their field. Jim's research shows that a company reaches success by targeting a goal, identifying a common enemy, setting up a role model, and achieving an internal transformation.

Want to become a Visible Expert like Jim Collins? Jim says passion, ambition, and humility are key. "The best leaders we've studied distinguish themselves first and foremost by their Level 5 ambition. Being fiercely ambitious for a cause or company larger than themselves, channeling ego into that larger goal, infused with the will to do whatever it takes to make good on that ambition."

### Step 4: Build Your Infrastructure

Every Visible Expert strategy requires a strong infrastructure, the everyday marketing materials and online tools you need to implement your strategy. Here are the basics you'll need to get started:

- *Profile Kit:* Your profile kit should contain professional headshots, a bio, and lists of your clients, awards, articles, and books.

- *Website:* Whether it's a dedicated bio page or blog on your firm's website, or a separate web domain altogether, you will need a sophisticated, professionally designed website. Your site should be easy to find in search engines and should integrate your blogging, video, and social channels. Whether or not to have a separate, personal website (in addition to your firm's website) is up to you and will depend on your target audience and the needs of your firm.

> You'll need a basic set of marketing materials and online tools to get started.

> "As an engineer and an artist, I knew my website would be crucial, as people would be judging my work through this channel. The website would be my portal to business, so it had to be professional, and it had to reflect my work. Today, I do little marketing and most of my leads find me through my website." —Robert Lang, internationally known Visible Expert and origami artist.

- *Speaking Engagement Page:* To encourage speaking engagements, your website should have a page dedicated to your experience in this area. This page should contain at least one video of you speaking, as well as links to your downloadable media kit.

- **Narrative Video:** In addition to your speaking page video, it's helpful to have a narrative video that gives viewers a peek at the real you. Ideally, this video will tell a story, conveying your credentials and experience through the testimony of others.

- **Social Profiles:** In Step 3, you identified social channels frequented by your audience. Now is the time to build out your profiles on those channels, making them as sophisticated as possible and integrating them with your website. Provide prominent links to all of your social channels so that it's easy for users to access and share your content. Keep your branding consistent across all platforms, including logos, graphical elements, and voice.

### Step 5: Develop Your Personal Skillset

In Step 2, you identified areas that needed improvement. Begin to address these areas now. Skill development is not a one-and-done activity. Instead, it will be a continual process of learning, practicing, and improving. Start at the basic level—for example, attending public speaking classes or hiring a social media coach.

Then incorporate these new skills into your daily routine. Ask for help whenever needed. And don't avoid your weaknesses—the goal is to become as well rounded as possible.

Skill development is not a one-and-done activity.

### Step 6: Grow Your Expert Brand

Congratulations! You've mapped out your strategy and built the infrastructure to support it. Everything is in place, and it's time to start executing your strategy. That means it's time to start producing content.

You might, for instance, consider a mix of blog posts, videos, and SlideShares. As you develop online content, be sure to employ keyword research and SEO techniques. And don't shy away from repurposing your content. That keynote address you delivered last month can be turned into a SlideShare and then reworked into a longer article that you send out to your email list. Reusing your content allows you to reach more people across more channels without doing a lot more work. Try it!

Your blog posts can be compiled into a book—in as little as six months.

Speaking of repurposing content, here's another secret to get you further faster. As you create your content, start thinking about the book you want to write. Many of those blog posts, articles, and SlideShares that you produce on a daily or weekly basis can be compiled and turned into a book—in as little as six months. And if you approach your day-to-day content with a book in mind, your writing will be more focused and meaningful.

In fact, this is exactly what content marketing guru Joe Pulizzi does. "I have a goal to write a book every two years," He says. "I use a blog-to-book strategy. I write one blog post per week for my company and one for LinkedIn. I think of blog posts as future book chapters, and that helps me stay focused."

**Step 7: Track and Adjust**

In your journey to the top, it's all too easy to get distracted by the doing and forget about the monitoring. But tracking your progress and making course corrections along the way is a critical part of the ascent. It's how you discover what works and what doesn't so that you can become a more efficient marketer. Every month or two, take a look at your key metrics. You'll be able to see if new activities are producing results and whether you need to make adjustments before you've wasted too much time.

> You'll need to analyze your individual tactics as well as your overall strategy.

You'll want to review a variety of metrics from your different channels, including lead sources, web traffic, conversions, number of leads, speaking opportunities, partnerships, and media mentions. And don't forget the big picture. You'll need to analyze not only the performance of your individual tactics, but also your overall strategy. Does your approach to the marketplace still make sense? Are you getting any traction? Are there opportunities you haven't considered?

## Starting the Ascent

Now that you have a program in hand, there's really nothing stopping you from becoming a Visible Expert—except, perhaps, your own doubts. In the final chapter, we will address some common concerns and obstacles that can stall an expert's ascent. After that, there's nothing left to do except start climbing.

## TAKEAWAYS

There are 7 steps in the Visible Expert program:

1. Candidate Selection—the ideal candidate balances practical factors with a soft skillset

2. Status Assessment—evaluate your current visibility level, as well as your strengths and weaknesses

3. Strategy Development—your strategy should focus on five key areas: Expertise, Audience, Visibility Tools, Promotional Channels, Resources and Support

4. Infrastructure—your marketing materials and online tools, including a website, head shots, bios, videos, and more

5. Personal Skillset—work hard to improve your areas of weakness and get help as you need it

6. Growing your *Expert Brand*—use content marketing to become more visible

7. Track and Adjust—regularly review your metrics and make adjustments to your strategy along the way

# Michael Graves

Michael Graves is a legend in the world of architecture and design. After earning a Master's in architecture from Harvard University in 1959, he quickly made a name for himself, winning five architecture competitions in a row and being recognized as one of the "New York Five"—a top representative and thought leader of New Urbanism and New Classical Architecture.

In 1999, Michael jumped into the mainstream with his revolutionary decision to partner with the chain department store, Target. The first high-end designer to make his products available to the average citizen, Michael became a household name overnight, turning a major profit for himself and exponentially boosting Target's cool-factor. Since then, his model of partnering with chain stores has been copied by many other high-end designers, from fashion to furniture.

In 2003, Michael was stricken with an infection that left him paralyzed from the waist down. His paralysis inspired him to dive into medically focused designs, re-imagining everything from crutches to hospitals. He even started designing homes for organizations like the Wounded Warrior Project and Habitat for Humanity.

Today, Michael Graves remains a managing principal of the two architecture and design firms that share his name, commissioning high-profile projects across the globe. He passes on his passion to the next generation by serving as the Robert Schirmer Professor of Architecture, Emeritus at Princeton University. By combining the fields of architecture and design into a niche all his own, Graves made it clear that he is one architect who cannot be boxed in.

REGOLA
FEUDALE
PASSO FEUDO
m. 2121

| | | |
|---|---|---|
| Rif. Torre di Pisa | 1.40 | |
| 516 Forcella dei Campanili | 2.50 | |
| Bivacco Latemar | 3.20 | |

| | | |
|---|---|---|
| Tresca | 0.30 | |
| Pelenzana – La Forcella | 1.30 | 515 |
| Predazzo | 4.00 | |

| | | |
|---|---|---|
| Malga Gardonè | 1.00 | |
| Al Fol | 2.10 | 504 |
| Predazzo | | |

BAITA CASERINA
BAR RISTORANTE
30 min                      515

**CHAPTER 10:**

# Final Considerations

By now we hope you understand the power of the Visible Expert. You've seen how these stars transfer credibility to a firm and—in the cases of Level 4 and 5 experts—are powerful enough to "make" a company or launch a new product or service line. You've learned that Visible Experts command the highest fees in the industry. You know what happens at every stage of the ascent, and you understand the steps you need to take to get there.

The results are in. And firms with Visible Experts are the clear winners. But even after seeing the results, you—or your firm—may still have a few doubts. It's natural and healthy to be skeptical. That's why we've written this last chapter. We hope it answers your biggest questions and concerns. If, after reading this chapter, you still have questions, feel free to contact us directly and we'll answer you promptly.

### 1. Can the Visible Expert program teach non-experts to become famous?

No. To become a Visible Expert, you must be an expert first. It is impossible to promote an expert brand if there is nothing behind that brand. As we saw in Chapter 3, Levels 1 and 2 of the Visible Expert ascent are focused on building expertise and establishing a niche. These steps are critical. In order for the Visible Expert program to work, professionals must have something of substance to offer their audience.

### 2. Will a Visible Expert undermine or overshadow my firm's brand?

Remember—there's nothing like having a Visible Expert on staff to turbocharge both a firm's reputation and marketplace visibility. From attracting higher fees, to accelerating growth and new business, Visible Experts are a boon to business on all fronts. Visible Experts and their firms build and enhance each other's brands, hand-in-hand. The star brings instant credibility and recognition to a firm while, in turn, the firm offers the star a vehicle for growth and expansion. It's a symbiotic relationship that benefits both parties.

> To become a Visible Expert, you *must* be an expert first.

However, if your firm is small and highly dependent on a single Visible Expert's fame (for instance, when Visible Experts found their own firms), diversifying is a good strategy for future growth. Consider starting a program to cultivate other Visible Experts in your firm. That way you can expand the power of your brand while minimizing the loss in prestige and income that can occur if a Visible Expert retires or leaves the firm.

> Visible Experts turbocharge a firm's reputation and visibility.

Here's how Visible Expert Joe Pulizzi addressed this challenge at the firm he founded: "When Content Marketing Institute was born, I leveraged as much of my personal brand as I could to launch the company. Initially, we had 'Joe' all over the site. But we've reduced that over time. Right now the two brands help bolster each other. But both brands also can stand on their own. The idea is that if Joe leaves, CMI can still exist."

### 3. Does becoming a Visible Expert mean I am pigeonholed into one specialty, forever?

As we learned in Chapter 7, carving out a niche does make it easier to become visible. While we recommend that you start out by focusing on a niche, you may not need to remain in it forever. In fact, being a Visible Expert makes it easier to move beyond your niche. At Level 4 or 5, Visible Experts enjoy a platform of visibility. At that point, they can decide to use the platform to publicize other areas of expertise.

This was the case for architect Michael Graves, who first made a name for himself with his award-winning postmodern designs. After reaching a high level of visibility in the world of architecture, Michael stepped outside his niche, bringing designs to mainstream America with a line of eye-catching housewares for Target, the chain department store. Now Michael has widened his scope once again. In the wake of an illness that left him paralyzed from the chest down, Michael has become the leading voice for design that accommodates disabilities and helps injured people heal. "Who knew that well-designed furniture and equipment could be part of the solution to reducing patient falls and the spread of infection?" Michael asks. For now, he has dedicated himself to being a major part of that solution.

**4. How do I choose a Visible Expert candidate? Isn't it unfair to promote some employees, and not others?**
To eliminate issues of fairness, consider creating a program that is available to any of your professional staff. If done well, your program can even become a great recruiting tool. The key is transparency, making it clear to all employees what is expected of a candidate. Remember that there is no such thing as too many Visible Experts. Empowering others to succeed will raise the value of your entire firm.

There are many great reasons to open up a Visible Expert program to everyone in your firm. *Here are just a few:*

- Making opportunity available to your professional staff leads to an open, transparent work environment where everyone knows what it takes to get ahead.

- Having a stable of Visible Experts at various levels multiplies the visibility of your entire firm across all of your stars.

- An established program allows you to see which staff members are taking advantage of available opportunities. It will quickly become obvious who wants to get ahead and who is happy to coast.

- When you have multiple Visible Experts in your firm, you lessen your risk if one star decides to leave.

- Having Visible Experts at different levels extends your firm's reach into different levels of the firms of prospective clients and teaming partners.

**5. Is it true that only the smartest and most original people can become Visible Experts?**

Visible Experts in our study consistently said they did not consider themselves the smartest or the most original minds in their fields. Instead, they are strategic and hardworking, homing in on a specialized topic or audience and then promoting themselves within that niche. They also are excellent communicators, with an ability to simplify complex topics for the benefit of clients, leads, and partners.

Hard work and a strategic focus are a Visible Expert's most important qualities.

There is nothing stopping you from becoming a Visible Expert. Using the strategies in this book, any competent professional can increase their visibility and cultivate their expertise. And now you now have the tools to get started.

### 6. What if I'm too busy to become a Visible Expert?

A firm's best people are always going to be busy with client work and other obligations. What sets Visible Experts apart is a strategic commitment to invest in their careers. Developing Visible Expert skills requires setting up a program and scheduling the time to make it happen.

Here's how architect Sarah Susanka made time for personal growth: "I recognized that writing was what I felt passionate about, but I had no space in my life to do it. And I was so busy with my architecture firm that if I didn't make some shift in my life, there would never be space for it. So I decided to pretend that I was my own client. I plugged myself into my own calendar and even gave myself a project number. I held myself to it, and that first book changed everything for me. All you have to do is take that one first, small step. It's amazing what happens when you focus yourself on something that you really want."

You can also take some of the burden off of your Visible Experts by retaining outside professionals to assist with their writing, blogging, social media, and other promotional activities. Of course, these activities cannot be completely segregated—a Visible Expert must stay engaged in these activities to maintain and grow their Visible Expert status.

Consider outside resources for writing, blogging, and social media.

### 7. Everyone wants to work with our experts, and it will only get worse if they become even more visible. How do we balance access?

Most clients will want to work with a Visible Expert. While this can be great for business, it can create competing demands. Especially at the higher levels of visibility, you'll need to set up a gatekeeping system. You also can regulate access to a Visible Expert by charging higher rates and by delegating responsibilities to a team. This is where the benefit

# Seth Godin

At the nexus of technology and marketing you'll find Seth Godin, prolific author, self-proclaimed heretic, and thought leader. With over 17 works in publication, including a *New York Times* bestseller, Seth managed to leverage his background in philosophy and computer science to craft a personal brand centered on trust and "tribes"—movements of true believers committed to a cause.

A rule breaker by definition, Seth has always done things just a little differently. His early success with Yoyodyne, the world's first Internet-based direct marketer, earned him $30 million and the vice presidency of direct marketing at Yahoo! in 1998. He used that momentum to found Squidoo, a community website that shared a portion of its profits with charity and another 50% with its contributors. The site later became one of the top 500 most-visited sites in the world.

Godin also has a history of guiding younger entrepreneurs as they pave their own roads to success. One of his more unique teaching ventures involved the creation of a six-month, alternative MBA program that required program applicants to actually interview one other before submitting a list of preferred future classmates.

When he's not traveling to speaking engagements or hosting his weekly podcast, Seth is probably writing articles for his blog—one of the most popular in the world. By staying true to his clients and spreading his brand through content marketing, Seth Godin is living proof that the world gives back to those brave enough to go their own way.

of the halo effect really kicks in—a Visible Expert will share the limelight, conveying credibility onto other team members who will share in the client work.

Here's how Chris Mercer handles this challenge at his firm. "I am Chairman of the Board of Directors at Mercer Capital, but I am no longer involved in the day-to-day operations. It frees up a lot of my time. Now I spend my time either working with clients or doing business development: writing, speaking, or giving testimony as an expert witness."

### 8. Will the Visible Expert's role change over time? How can we plan for the future?

As we saw in Chapter 3, each level of visibility brings changes in a Visible Expert's role and focus. That means experts will need to adapt as they ascend. Visible Experts must continuously examine and adjust what they do with their time so they can make the most efficient use of their time and expertise. As they become more visible in the marketplace, they can expect to do less direct client work and more strategy, planning, large-scale promotional events, and teaching of other team members.

People want to stay at firms where they can grow their own careers.

"The dynamic changes as your visibility increases," explains Alan Weiss, internationally recognized speaker, author, and CEO of Summit Consulting. "You become less of a doer, and more of an advisor. As you gain authority you can operate at your own level. You can have people come to you, for instance. Now, if people want a consulting session, they come see me here at my home in Newport."

**9. What if my firm develops Visible Experts and they end up leaving?**
Employees come and go—it comes with the territory. However, there are several things you can do to mitigate this risk:

- When selecting new staff, choose individuals with an eye to the future. Ask candidates about their future plans, and choose people who care about helping you and your firm grow.

- Create opportunity. People want to stay at firms where they can grow their own careers. Investing in a Visible Expert program signals that you care about team members' career development.

- Losing a Visible Expert doesn't have to mean your firm will fall apart. If you develop multiple Visible Experts you won't be putting all of your eggs in one basket.

- Leverage the halo effect. As you strengthen the firm's overall brand you reduce the risk of losing a Visible Expert.

## Making the Case

Visible Experts are one of the business world's best-kept secrets. And for the first time, the blueprints are available to everyone. We've broken down the Visible Expert process to its essentials, and now anyone with sufficient ambition and tenacity can replicate it. By following the example set by the Fast Trackers in our study, it's possible to achieve visibility even faster.

We hope this book inspires you and your colleagues to reach higher and make the most of your talents. Success has never been so attainable. As you set out for the summit, we encourage you to share your stories with us. Who knows? You might read about yourself in the next edition of this book.

## TAKEAWAYS

- To become a Visible Expert, you must be an expert first.

- A Visible Expert can turbocharge a firm's reputation and visibility in the marketplace.

- Once Visible Experts reach Level 4 or 5, they can expand beyond their niche.

- There is no such thing as too many Visible Experts. Empowering others to succeed will raise the value of your entire firm.

- Hard work, strategic thinking, and focus are a Visible Expert's most important qualities.

- Schedule time for Visible Expert development and allocate team support to help with promotional activities.

- Regulate access to high-level Visible Experts by charging higher rates and by delegating responsibilities to a team.

- As Visible Experts become more visible in the marketplace, they can expect to do less direct client work and more strategy.

- Mitigate loss by developing multiple Visible Experts in your firm.

# Tim Ash

Over the past year, Tim Ash, founder and CEO of SiteTuners, spoke at 18 different industry events. The year before that, it was 24. Maintaining his status as a Visible Expert in the field of website conversion and optimization means that Tim has to share his knowledge widely. But when he started out, he had no idea that his ideas would turn into something so big.

Tim was grinding through the end of a doctoral program in computer science when he suddenly realized he was on the wrong track. So he left academia and dove head first into entrepreneurship. 18 years and three startups later, Tim says, "It's been quite the rollercoaster ride. But I realized I liked carving my own path. Think of it this way: If you're not the lead dog, the view is always going to be the same."

Like many Visible Experts, Tim's status was sparked by the success of a book, *Landing Page Optimization*, published in 2008. After his book hit the shelves, he received a flood of prospective clients—and a newly minted reputation. He says, "The book is the best $12 business card I've ever had. There's nothing like getting a signed copy from the author to help advance the sale."

Tim also credits his success to specialization. He says, "My company needed to be able to say: *we only do this*. So we don't do SEO, we don't build websites, we don't do PPC, and we don't touch coding or web development. There is more than enough to keep up with just in our narrow niche."

# Additional Resources

## Books

**Inside the Buyer's Brain**
www.hingemarketing.com/library/article/book-inside-the-buyers-brain

**Professional Services Marketing**
www.hingemarketing.com/library/article/professional_services_marketing_book_free_chapter

**Online Marketing for Professional Services**
www.hingemarketing.com/library/article/online_marketing_for_professional_services

**Spiraling Up: How to Create a High Growth, High Value Professional Services Firm**
www.hingemarketing.com/spiralingup

## Guide

**Becoming a Visible Expert℠: A Guide for Professional Services Executives**
www.hingemarketing.com/library/article/becoming_a_visible_expert_a_guide_for_professional_services_executives

## Research Report

**Visible Experts℠: How High Visibility Expertise Helps Professionals, Their Firms, and Their Clients**
www.hingemarketing.com/library/article/beyond-referrals-how-todays-buyers-check-you-out

## Online Resources

**Professional Services Marketing Today**
Keep up with the latest research and get the practical marketing advice you need to take your professional services firm to new heights.
www.hingemarketing.com/blog
RSS Feed: http://feeds.feedblitz.com/hingemarketing

**Pivot Newsletter**
Subscribe to Hinge's pivotal briefings on brand marketing for professional services firms, delivered monthly to your inbox.
www.hingemarketing.com/pivot

**Professional Services Executive Forum**
Join the leading online forum for leaders and marketers of professional services firms. Discuss the latest issues in marketing, research, strategy, and business development with experts and peers.
www.linkedin.com/groups/Professional-Services-Executive-Forum-3828540/about

### Learn More About Our Visible Expert Program

Hinge's Visible Expert Program helps firms and individuals develop a strategy to expand brand recognition, increase leads, and accelerate growth through the cultivation of in-house Visible Experts. From a research-based assessment of current Visible Expert status, to implementation of strategy, our team of experts has you covered — every step of the way.

For more information, call 703.391.8870 or email us at info@hingemarketing.com.

# About the Authors

**Lee W. Frederiksen, Ph.D., Managing Partner, Hinge**

Lee is an award-winning marketer and renowned business strategist who helped pioneer the field of research-driven marketing. As the Managing Partner of Hinge, he draws on his Ph.D. in behavioral psychology and his entrepreneurial experience as CEO of three successful firms to help clients achieve high growth and profitability.

Lee has worked with a number of global brands, including American Express, Time Life, Capital One, Monster.com, and Yahoo! He's been quoted in a number of mainstream publications and he regularly speaks at major industry events around the country.

Lee led the research studies that form the basis of this book. He is also a co-author of *Inside the Buyer's Brain: How to Turn Buyers into Believers*; *Spiraling Up: How to Create a High Growth, High Value Professional Services Firm*; *Online Marketing for Professional Services*; and *Professional Services Marketing, Second Edition*.

lfrederiksen@hingemarketing.com
www.linkedin.com/in/leefrederiksen

**Elizabeth Harr, Partner, Hinge**

Elizabeth specializes in helping technology firms grow. After co-founding a tech firm that provided Microsoft solutions, she moved on to work with clients in the for-profit, non-profit, and government sectors, helping them map out growth plans using technology adoption. Elizabeth draws on a decade's experience in strategic planning, communications, and alliance development in her role as Partner and Account Director at Hinge.

Elizabeth is also a co-author of *Inside the Buyer's Brain: How to Turn Buyers into Believers*. When she's not working with clients to increase growth and profitability, you'll find her writing articles and book chapters, conducting webinars, and speaking at industry events. She holds a Master's degree in International Economics from Columbia University.

eharr@hingemarketing.com
www.linkedin.com/in/eharr

## Sylvia Montgomery, CPSM, Senior Partner, Hinge

A specialist in the A/E/C industry, Sylvia draws on 20 years' experience in business and marketing to help firms achieve growth and position themselves in the marketplace. As Senior Partner and Account Director at Hinge, Sylvia spends her days working with clients and managing the Architecture, Engineering and Construction team, when she is not speaking at industry events around the country.

Co-author of *Inside the Buyer's Brain: How to Turn Buyers into Believers* and *Online Marketing for Professional Services*, and the author of numerous articles, white papers, and webinars, Sylvia is also an active member of Society for Marketing Professional Services (SMPS-DC), where she held a seat on the board of directors. She holds degrees from University of Maryland University College, George Washington University, and Trinity University.

smontgomery@hingemarketing.com
www.linkedin.com/in/sylviamontgomery
twitter.com/BrandStrong

# About Hinge &
# Hinge Research Institute

Hinge is a leading branding and marketing firm for the professional services. Our original research on high-growth firms and professional services buyers helps clients grow faster and be more profitable.

Hinge provides a complete suite of services, including Visible Expert[SM] development, research and strategy, brand development, comprehensive online marketing programs, award-winning creative, content marketing, and lead-generating websites. Hinge works with firms around the world with a special focus on architecture, engineering, construction, accounting, technology, management consulting, and legal services.

The firm's research division, the Hinge Research Institute, studies high-growth professional services firms and their clients. Visit Hinge's extensive library of research reports, books and other publications at www. hingemarketing.com/library.

For more information about Hinge's services, please contact us:

**Hinge**
12030 Sunrise Valley Drive, Suite 120
Reston, VA 20191
703.391.8870
info@hingemarketing.com

CPSIA information can be obtained at www.ICGtesting.com
Printed in the USA
LVIW01n1041171114
414083LV00002B/2